A VISION
OF THE
DEEP

A VISION
OF THE
DEEP

Uncovering the Treasure of Life in Christ

SUSAN SCOTT SUTTON

PUBLICATIONS

Fort Washington, PA 19034

A Vision of the Deep

Published by CLC Publications

ISBN: 978-0-87508-786-3
Copyright 2009 Susan Scott Sutton

U.S.A.
P.O. Box 1449, Fort Washington, PA 19034

GREAT BRITAIN
51 The Dean, Alresford, Hants, SO24 9BJ

AUSTRALIA
P.O. Box 2299, Strathpine, QLD 4500

NEW ZEALAND
10 MacArthur Street, Feilding

Unless otherwise noted, all Scripture quotations are from
  Holy Bible, New International Version, copyright © 1973, 1978, 1984
    by International Bible Society.
  Used by permission of Zondervan Bible Publishers.

Italicized words in Scripture quotes are the emphasis of the author.

This printing 2009

Printed in the United States of America

To Scott, Susan and Elisabeth

You lived these stories and
gleaned your own treasures from desert places.

Make us thy mountaineers—
We would not linger on the lower slope.
Fill us afresh with hope, O God of Hope,
That undefeated we may climb the hill
As seeing Him who is invisible.

Let us die climbing. When this little while
Lies far behind us and the last defile
Is all alight, and in that light we see
Our Leader and our Lord—what will it be?

(Amy Carmichael)[1]

Contents

Part One

Catching the Vision

Part Two

Living the Deeper Life

Acknowledgements

A book is like a child. You put into it what you know and do your best with what you have. You make mistakes. You indulge too much in some areas; you worry too much in others.

Throughout the shaping and molding, you keep pouring in, keep praying, keep hoping that the final product, despite your imperfect efforts, will be good. That someone out there will love it as much as you have. You never feel your work is completely over, you feel keenly you could have done a better job—but at some point you have to let it go into the wide world. You have to let it be what it is, no longer yours to mold, correct, edit or attempt to change.

As a parent, you are always glad for others who care as much for your children as you do. You're especially glad when they pray with you. I asked several special women in my life to pray regularly for my writing, and I cannot thank each one enough for saying yes and for actually praying: my daughters Susan and Elisabeth, my daughter-in-law Sarah and my special friends Miriam, Sheila, Leslie, Lisa and Linda. There were many on staff at WEC headquarters where we live who prayed and, even more, encouraged me to hide away to write. In many ways, this book is as much yours as mine, because you have prayed it to completion.

And thank you, my daughter Susan, for regularly sending me quotes about writing that kept me smiling, kept my perspective right and kept me going.

When I tell stories from Chad, they are, more often than not, my husband's stories. He tells them better than I write them. Thank you, Louis, for letting me share your stories and for encouraging my attempts to record the truths you gleaned from them.

Finally, I have to say a special thanks to Becky English, my editor with CLC. You are wonderfully patient, encouraging, flexible and capable—a joy to know and to work with.

Letter to the Reader

Many people have said things worth remembering. I have numerous books filled with memorable words—sentences and paragraphs that grab my attention as I read. Wanting to keep them in mind, I transfer them to personal journals. Then most are forgotten as soon as I write them down. They lie in literary exile until I vaguely recall that someone put a certain truth in so apt a way (what *was* it?) and begin a feverish search, turning page after page and condemning myself for not categorizing things better.

Some quotes, however, resist exile. They burn themselves unforgettably on my heart. Refusing to go away, they shape my thinking, and therefore my life, forever after. One is from Antoine de Saint-Exupéry, best-known for his children's classic, *The Little Prince*. Saint-Exupéry wrote these insightful words:

> If you want to build a ship, don't just gather men to collect wood, divide the work and give orders. Rather, teach them to long for the immensity of the sea.[1]

This speaks of vision and passion and, at the same time, of meaning and motivation for what we do in life. Without a vision of the sea, building a ship has no meaning. Without passion, collecting wood has no motivation other than duty.

But given a vision greater than the work, motivation naturally follows. Collecting wood is no longer a duty but a desire.

This advice would do well for management seminars, but I think it is equally relevant for our spiritual lives. I am afraid that many church members, at least in the West, are busy with the Christian life but have lost a vision for life with Christ.

Some are content with merely doing assigned tasks—building the ship, so to speak. But others feel restless. They are faithful in church involvement. They diligently practice personal and corporate spiritual disciplines such as Bible study, prayer and fasting. Yet they feel somehow that these are touching only the surface of their lives. *There must be something more than this*, they think.

They are right. There is more to being a Christian than doing all the things a Christian is supposed to do. There is a much greater reason for being involved at church than keeping programs and committees running smoothly.

Building a boat for the sake of building a boat reveals limited vision. When you finish, you have . . . a boat. But building a boat because you long for the sea—and because you need a boat to get there—brings passion and commitment, even joy, to the smallest and most menial of tasks.

Activities and spiritual disciplines have a purpose. They have meaning because they take us somewhere we want to go. If they didn't, we would do well to stay home on Sundays. There are other things to do with our time, other clubs we can join if we want community and activity.

Weariness with meaningless activity is, I suspect, one reason many people hop from church to church or stop attending altogether. Their vision of the Christian life is limited to external practices of faith.

Two things can happen when we become dissatisfied with our experience of Christianity. We can discard practices of the faith. In other words, we can stop collecting wood since we have no vision of the sea. Or we can recognize that something significant is happening. We can pay attention to the restlessness and understand where it comes from.

"You have created us for yourself, and our heart cannot be stilled until it finds rest in you," wrote Augustine in the early fifth century. His words resonate with us today, because they are true. The heart is made for more than simply collecting wood. It is made for the immensity of the sea.

"Deep calls to deep," the psalmist writes (Ps. 42:7). Our restlessness comes from God Himself reaching out to us, stirring up dissatisfaction, because He has indeed created us for more than commonplace experience. He created us for Himself—to be in relationship with Him and to bear His image.

The heart knows this. The heart longs for this. The heart is forever restless until it rests in Him. That is why so few things in life completely satisfy us, why we are always looking for another church or another experience or another person or another possession. We are attempting to fill the deep place of soul satisfaction reserved for God alone.

The world has philosophies, religions and creeds aplenty. But God, through Christ, offers us Himself. Religions and ideals do not walk with us through the hard places of life. A Person goes with us, a living Person with whom we can talk and cry and laugh through the ups and downs of life. Codes of behavior do not motivate change. But a relationship with

Someone we care about deeply, and who we now know cares deeply about us, motivates us to live rightly—not just because we should, but because we want to.

I would not trade life with Christ or the lessons He has taught me for any lesser life in the world. I have *often* been a slow learner. But God is, thankfully, very patient with His children. I can truly echo the words of Teresa of Ávila, "May God be forever blessed for putting up with me for so long. Amen."

This book is my imperfect attempt to give you a vision of the deep. It offers lessons of life with Christ: the deeper life of a heart set free, transformed by His Spirit from the inside out. Each of these lessons is a treasure of this hidden life with Christ—whether learned on the edge of the Sahara where my family served for thirteen years or in suburban America where we now live at our mission headquarters. My prayer is that once you have finished the last chapter, you will have found new treasures, or rediscovered old ones, for your own journey with Christ.

No one has more vision and passion for us than God does. May He stir in you a longing for the immensity of the sea—a longing that is, in reality, for Him. May He show you life as it is meant to be lived—Life with a capital L—for Him, with Him and in His way.

Susan Scott Sutton
2008

Part One

Catching the Vision

The kingdom of heaven is like treasure hidden in a field.
When a man found it, he hid it again, and then in his
joy went and sold all he had and bought that field.
(*Matthew 13:44*)

-1-

Engagements of the Heart

Since he looked upon me my heart is not my own.
He hath run away to heaven with it. (*Samuel Rutherford*)

You will seek me and find me when you seek me
with all your heart. (*Jeremiah 29:13*)

Years ago—more years than I
care to count now—three friends and I declared our undying love for the most beautiful animal on earth by forming the Horse Lovers Club. We held meetings in our back yards, read *Misty of Chincoteague* and *The Black Stallion* series, and vowed always to love horses and never to shave our legs. At the same time we formed a Boy Haters Club, just as passionate in its intent. As the years progressed, however, so did our exceptions to the boys on our "objectionable" list. This club eventually, and not surprisingly, floundered due to lack of interest.

Over time the first one folded, as well. We grew out of a fascination with horses and into a fascination with boys (and consequently retracted our vow never to shave our legs). To mark this passage from childhood to what we considered more mature interests, we formed a new fan club for a then-popular group, the Monkees.

Throwing our preteen hearts just as passionately into this new enthrallment, Jane, Carol, Jenny and I faithfully read everything about Davy, Mickey, Peter and Mike. We each had our favorite (mine was Peter), memorized their song lyrics as devotedly as we had formerly studied horses, and we imitated our new interests, walking with locked arms and crossing legs—getting "the funniest looks from everyone we meet . . . hey, hey, we're the Monkees!"

Eventually, this club too met its end. We adored those four guys on a screen, but it was a distant adoration. There was little to keep our hearts engaged when other, more immediate interests claimed our time and attention. The attraction was fun while it lasted, but, going the way of its predecessors, it faded in relevance to our lives.

The Problem with Clubs

Horses, boy hating and the Monkees held several things in common for a group of girls growing up in North Carolina in the late sixties. They engaged our hearts for a moment in time. They gave us a sense of belonging and identity. And they satisfied a longing to be part of something outside ourselves.

Every longing of the heart has its roots in a God-planted desire—one He meant to satisfy ultimately with Himself. But the world has lost its way since the creation, and our inclinations have gone askew. The Enemy of our souls has either twisted them into wrong appetites, or he has convinced us to seek fulfillment of reasonable and good desires in wrong places.

One of our God-given desires is a longing to be part of something bigger than ourselves. He created us for something outside ourselves—which is, of course, life with Him— but having forgotten why we were created, we look for someone else to live for or something else to satisfy us.

This may well be why fan clubs exist in such abundance. Shared adoration satisfies our longing to be part of something bigger as well as our desire to belong. Identification with something greater than us can even influence behavior, proven by a Monkees imitation that only

I was in danger of losing my faith—at least, what faith I could claim at the time.

besotted preteen girls could care to copy. Belonging to something or someone at a given moment in time declares to the world, "This is who I am!"

The problem with fan clubs is that they depend on members—and fans are notoriously fickle. As a result, horses, boy hating and a sixties' pop group now have something else in common for that group of girls: They are no longer part of our lives. We grew up. We moved on to other interests. Our hearts turned elsewhere.

Hearts without an Anchor

As a teenager in the seventies, my tendency to lose interest in progressive fads had the makings of an unhealthy habit—a habit that could possibly cause me to discard something that touched deeper matters of eternity. In my youthful understanding of spirituality, I was in danger of losing my faith—at least, what faith I could claim at the time.

Church had been a part of my life from the time I was first entrusted to nursery helpers on Sunday mornings. I grew up knowing the lingo and all the Bible stories. Today I very much appreciate a childhood in which church was a constant in our family life; but when my teenage years hit, things got difficult. I began the Search for meaning and significance that happens necessarily, and often painfully, in adolescence.

With typical teenage angst, I wrote poems questioning the meaning of life and seriously wondered if the answer was just "blowin' in the wind," as Bob Dylan so soulfully sang. *I*, at least, was blowing in the wind, drifting along on unsteady currents with no anchor to keep me in one place. Longing to be "myself" but not knowing who that was, I looked to my friends to determine who I should be and how I should act. Since they were drifting along in their own currents of uncertainty, this was not helpful. Adolescents do not make steady anchors for each other. *Who am I? Why am I here? What is the world all about?* These were questions of the heart that we were all flinging to the stars.

During this period of questioning, I never thought to look to the church for answers. God was already part of my life. I had "been there, done that," and was still doing it as far as attendance went. Infant-baptized, Sunday School-taught and a youth group regular, I had the religious side of life figured out. Or so I thought.

What I didn't know at the time was that although church was part of my life, God Himself was not—at least not in the way He intends to be. An actual relationship with God at that time was as nonexistent as a relationship with Peter York of the Monkees. The distantly adored Peter was just an image on a screen and a face in a magazine. At least in his case, I had a picture in mind when I thought of him. I had no idea what God looked like. To me He was as impersonal as a character in a book—to be believed in, respected and worshiped, but not known.

Thinking I had all that was possibly available in the God department, I never reached out to Him to fill the longings of my searching heart.

"Deep calls to deep," says the psalmist (Ps. 42:7).

Thankfully, He reached out to me.

Life with a Capital L

In my sixteenth year something happened that changed me—and is changing me still. I fell in love. It was an engagement of the heart so deep and real that it ended the Search. It connected my heart to the Jesus I had heard about every week for most of my childhood, but had never met personally until then. My perception of Him changed: No longer a character in a book, He became a living Person I could know.

"Ha!" you say. "I knew it. Of course." Well, *I* didn't know it. There was no "of course" in my teenage heart when the connection happened. I was clueless about knowing God up close and personal—that having a relationship with Him was the key to finding everything my heart longed for.

I remember well the time and place that everything changed and Life with a capital L began. The seed of this change was planted by a new group I had joined in high school called Young Life. Yet another club. The difference with this one was in its leaders; they were college students who clearly had not outgrown their heart engagement. In fact, they seemed to be growing more and more into it. They were downright passionate about Christ, who was the focus of their gatherings. They were passionate enough to travel thirty minutes every week from a major state university to a rural high school and spend time with a group of adolescents drifting along in our various currents.

Outwardly I looked pretty good, but inwardly the restlessness remained.

To our parents, Young Life was a wholesome group that meant evenings in which they didn't have to worry about what we were up to. But to us it was an ocean that all of our unanchored hearts longed to move toward, because we saw in the staff something greater and more real than we had in our own lives.

During the course of that year, I watched the leaders. To them it was serious stuff to be a Christian. Following Christ went beyond the walls of church. Their God connection spilled over into the days of the week beyond Sundays. They spoke as if they knew God, and as if He touched every part of their lives.

Hmmm, I thought. *I should be more serious about my faith. After all, I am a Christian; I should start acting like one.* So I did. I carried my Bible around and even began to read it outside of Young Life meetings. I joined a prayer group. I joined a Bible study. I paid more attention in church. I worked on being friendlier, not just to my friends, but to everyone.

It was behavior modification at its best, and I had a miserable year. Outwardly I looked pretty good by stepping up my Christian behavior, but inwardly the restlessness remained. It not only remained—it grew. Dissatisfaction with what I saw in the world, which had prompted my search, deepened to dissatisfaction with what I saw in myself. *Maybe, I thought, the world isn't the problem.*

Trying to do the things a good Christian should only made me keenly aware that I was not a good Christian. I was not the loving, caring, patient, spiritual person that I hoped others perceived, and I had an increasing sense that God saw through the image I was trying to project.

He did, of course. The One who sees everything knows what is in the heart He created. I now realize that it was God's determined love and infinite grace that allowed my growing internal dissatisfaction. He had something to tell me, so He brought me to a place where I was ready to hear it.

"You Are Here"

Lao-Tzu, a Chinese philosopher who lived in the sixth century BC, wrote, "A journey of a thousand miles begins with a single step." A modern-day rendition is written on a T-shirt I bought at a spiritual formation seminar by Larry Crabb. It reads in bold lettering, "Every journey begins with a red dot." Dr. Crabb's point is that we need to know where we are before we can get to where we want to be.

The red dot on a map is extremely important, especially in this day of mega conference centers and super malls. Whether I am looking for a seminar room or a store, I head for a map. The first thing I locate is my destination; then I look for the red dot beside the words, "You are here." I cannot reach the place I want to go in the vast labyrinth of a mega mall unless I know two locations: where I want to be and where I am. Both are necessary for the journey.

In the same way, to get where we want to be with God we need to locate our spiritual "red dot," that place of soul-honesty that says, "Here I am, God." He knows, of course, where we are. Doubting, hurting, angry, confused, afraid, prideful, struggling with an area of sin . . . Our true state of heart and mind may be hidden from those around us, but not from God. And yet we are afraid to be honest with Him.

> *God is the safest place we can go with our true selves, because He knows us more than anyone ever can.*

I sometimes wonder what would have happened if Adam and Eve had been honest with God at their point of failure—if, instead of hiding from Him, they had run to Him as the One who knew them completely and still loved them unconditionally. His knowledge of them included their potential for wrong choices, but He still loved them absolutely. If they had not covered up their true selves, but had told God everything that had happened—including their doubt of His word and lack of trust in His love—I believe the conversation would have been different.

God is the safest place we can go with our true selves, because He knows us more than anyone ever can. Yet we swallow the Enemy's lie that God cannot be believed or trusted. Instead of being real, we cover up, just as Adam and Eve tried to do.

I was about to meet with the real God, not as a distant figure of Sunday School lessons and ideals to emulate but as He is: the living God who created me for life with Him. I was to learn that the real God wants the real me. He is not interested in outward shows of behavior and activities but in inward connections of the heart.

What happens when the real you meets the real God? Real transformation.

The Heart Finds Its Way Home

The actual location where God met me was at Windy Gap, a Young Life retreat center in the mountains of North Carolina.

A Young Life retreat means days of exhausting fun (keeping all those hormones at bay) and nights of spiritual challenge. On Saturday evening we gathered for the main message of the weekend. One hundred-plus students who were packed into the Windy Gap conference room heard a compelling message of God's love, of Christ's sacrifice on the cross and of His right to our lives. At the end of the message, we were encouraged to reflect on what we had just heard.

The message hit home for me, and I wanted to be alone. So I moved outside the conference hall, found a rock beside a small stream and sat down.

I had never heard so clearly and personally what God in His love had done for me.[1] His *ahab* (pursuing love) had to open my eyes before I could see that I was made for something more than I was experiencing—that all my questions found their answers in Him. His *hesed* (merciful and compassionate love) had to do something about the sin that kept me disconnected from the source of true Life.[2] Both aspects of divine love—God's passionate commitment to us and His compassionate mercy toward us—are seen most clearly in Christ on the cross.

Everything within me knew this was true, but I also knew that I was trying to live the Christian life, and it wasn't working. Selfishness, criticism, pride, insecurities and concern for the approval of others still ran rampant in my life. With the message of God's love and of the cross ringing in my ears, and with a desperation to be free of my "self" that was not what I wanted it to be, I cried out to God, "I've tried! I can't live the Christian life. I can't be good enough. I can't do this!"

Deep Truth responded to deep honesty with these words: "Good, I've been waiting for you to come to this point. Now we can begin."

Using words from the message, the Holy Spirit wove truth into my heart. "I know you can't do it. That's why I came. That's the reason for the cross. Now stop trying to do it on your own and start living Life as it is meant to be lived—with My Life in you and through you. Surrender your life to Me, and let's live this Life together. Let Me introduce myself—I am Jesus, and I am the One your heart is searching for."

The proverbial light bulb went on. I saw that what was missing in my life was Christ Himself. I had actually been living Christianity without Christ. It's not that my efforts hadn't been sincere. God truly was becoming more important to me, and living for Him was increasingly a desire of my heart. But even in my stepped-up version of Christianity, Jesus remained a distant figure I was trying to emulate.

The "red dot" reality revealed that I was still the star of my own show, so to speak. Life was still about me:

> Me trying to be a good person,
>> Me trying to be a better Christian,
>>> Me trying to "live for God."

There was a great deal of "me" in my life and little of Christ Himself. I understood now that I was meant to bear His image, not project my own.

That night I talked with God. It was not the first time I had prayed, but it was the night that my prayers changed from ritual to conversation. It was the night that eternity stepped once more into time, and God, through His son Jesus, reclaimed a soul that was made for Him, quieting the restless heart of a teenage girl sitting on a rock by a mountain stream.

The universe settled into place, and I felt as if I had come home. I *had* come home—to Someone. The One who created me, died for me, loved me for myself and sought me for Himself now welcomed me into His embrace.

Some would say I accepted Christ into my life for the first time that night. Others would declare that the Jesus I had believed in as Savior now became my Lord. Both of these are true. The living Christ did enter my life when I understood that Christianity is not my attempt to live that life, but Christ Himself living in and through me, doing what I cannot do on my own. Christ also, at that point, became a Lord to follow rather than an ideal to emulate.

But I say that deeper things happened when the real me met the real God. A member of a club became a member of a family. An image projector became an image bearer. A restless heart found its anchor. A soul found its way home.

Over thirty years later, I can say unwaveringly that Jesus' words that night have proven true. Going through life with Christ is an engagement of the heart so strong that I have never grown out of it. Like those Young Life leaders, I have grown *into* it more and more, because love, if it is genuine, only matures as the years go on.

Heart Beats

The heart that listens:

God looked into my heart as a teenager and knew all that was in it. This is not surprising.

The heart is designed for God:

> Ecclesiastes 3:11
> Deuteronomy 5:7; 30:15–20
> Isaiah 43:7, 21

The heart is God's measure of who we are:

> 1 Samuel 16:7
> 1 Chronicles 28:9
> 2 Chronicles 6:28–31

The heart is God's focus for change:

> Jeremiah 24:7
> Jeremiah 32:38–39

Ezekiel 11:19–20
Ezekiel 36:24–28

The heart that responds:

- How do you feel about God knowing everything that is on your heart at any moment? How honest do you feel you can be with Him? With others?
- What is your spiritual and emotional "red dot" in reference to life with God?
- Spend time with the Lord. Tell Him honestly where you are at this moment in life and in your walk with Him.

Part Two

Living the Deeper Life

God nowhere tells us to give up things for the sake of
giving them up. He tells us to give them up for the sake
of the only thing worth having . . . life with Himself.
(*Oswald Chambers*)[1]

−2−

Surrendering

Many are willing that Christ should be something, but few will consent that Christ should be everything. (*Alexander Moody Stuart*)

In the same way, any of you who does not give up everything he has cannot be my disciple. (*Luke 14:33*)

*I*n the beginning He was a public relations dream: thirty-something and dynamic; confident, yet humble; refreshingly unconventional. Just what the crowds liked. And if one could judge by numbers, they definitely liked the new rabbi who stepped outside the synagogues to perform miracles in the streets.

His name was Jesus, He came from Nazareth and He was amazing. More and more people gathered wherever He appeared to see if what they had heard about Him was true. And no one was disappointed.

He could make demons obey His commands. He could heal diseases, crippling ones and chronic ones, with nothing more than a word or a touch of His hand. He had actually restored sight to the blind and brought the dead back to life. What's more, He never charged for His services!

Besides such awesome displays of power, Jesus had a compelling authority in His teaching. On the hillsides and in the synagogues, He taught truth about God in a way that reached below the surface of conventional religion. It penetrated to the heart. At times He so skillfully debated against religious authorities that they had to back down, humiliated, in their arguments against Him. People were delighted (see Luke 13:17, for example).

But there was more. Instead of courting people of influence, the young and increasingly popular rabbi surrounded Himself with the decidedly *un*influential. His closest friends were ordinary people, hands-to-the-fishing-net working men and civil servants. In fact, He sought not only the company of ordinary people but of some definite undesirables in society. He never deliberately sought the company of the powerful, the attractive or the important. They came to Him.

If Jesus of Nazareth was aiming for success in life, He had a very unusual way of going about it.

Unconventional in His methods.
  Uncompromising in His teaching.
    Unconcerned with the opinions of others.

With such a fascinating public image, it is not surprising that crowds began to gather wherever Jesus went.

Crowd Control

I used to envision Jesus traveling from town to town with a small, select band of disciples. When He occasionally preached to larger numbers, in my mind it was a gathering of curious locals who made their way to the foot of a hill on the edge of town as Jesus was passing through. The people found places to sit on the ground, nudged their neighbors for quiet and then listened in rapt attention to the traveling rabbi—all very quiet and orderly.

This must surely have happened on occasion, but it is not the full picture. A good look through the Gospel accounts reveals that as Jesus' prominence grew, so did the need for crowd control. People went to great lengths to see Jesus, and they were not always polite in their efforts. Sometimes they surrounded houses and blocked doorways. One group destroyed the roof of someone's home in a desperate attempt to get His attention. Others commandeered boats and rowed across lakes. At one point the numbers became so large and unmanageable that people were trampling each other (see Mark 1:33, 2:2; Luke 12:1; John 6:24).

This frenzied pursuit is more like the behavior of celebrity devotees or European sports enthusiasts than quiet followers of a local rabbi. No wonder the religious and political leaders were getting nervous.

The Gospel of Luke, in particular, records the progression of Jesus' acclaim. We can trace His rise from a new face in the synagogues to a public figure of such proportion that if He were on the scene today, the media would have paparazzi assigned permanently to a "Jesus watch." Observe how His following expanded:

> Jesus returned to Galilee in the power of the Spirit, and *news about him spread* through the whole countryside. He taught in their synagogues, and everyone praised him. (4:14–15)

Yet the news about him spread all the more, so that *crowds of people came to hear him* and to be healed of their sicknesses. (5:15)

Soon afterward, Jesus went to a town called Nain, and his disciples and *a large crowd went along with him.* (7:11)

Meanwhile, *when a crowd of many thousands had gathered, so that they were trampling on one another,* Jesus began to speak. (12:1)

Large crowds were traveling with Jesus. (14:25)

Can you sense the momentum? People are so fascinated with Jesus that far more than twelve men attach themselves to Him. Vast numbers, hungry and restless for healing or for a hero, have left their homes to be with Him. What a reception. Such popularity would make any modern public relations firm rub its hands together in holy glee.

Yes, Jesus, would have been a promotional dream if He had allowed his notoriety to continue. But an interesting thing happened . . .

Yes, Jesus, would have been a promotional dream if He had allowed this growing notoriety to continue. He was making a name for Himself and was on His way to becoming the most talked-about religious figure in the nation. He had a following of huge proportions. But an interesting thing happened along the way.

As His popularity grew, Jesus withdrew more and more from the crowds. He actually seemed intent on working *against* fame and recognition. If He had wanted admirers,

He would have made a greater effort to impress the multitudes. He would have performed more miracles. He would have chosen His words more carefully. Instead, He began to say things that turned listeners away. At these moments, Jesus seemed determined to make it harder rather than easier for people to stay with Him.

More Than a Crowd Pleaser

Chapter 14 of Luke's Gospel records one such time. At a crucial point that seems the height of Jesus' fame as far as crowd size suggests, He told the people around Him what He required of His disciples.

Picture this. You are present at the moment recorded by Luke: "Large crowds were traveling with Jesus, and turning to them he said . . ." (14:25).

Imagine you are one of Jesus' disciples, and you are sitting near Him. You believe He is the greatest thing to happen since the days of Elijah, a prophet who performed miracles and brought Israel back to the true worship of God. You want everyone else to believe the same, but you realize there are people in the throng not yet sure what they think. You also know that lurking in the shadows are critics who would love nothing more than to find something to bring Him down.

You see Jesus turning to the mass of humanity before Him. What would you want Him to say to all these people? Perhaps He should thank everyone for coming. After all, they have gone through quite a bit of trouble to be here. People like to feel appreciated. If you could whisper in His ear, you might advise Him to say something warm and welcoming, maybe even begin with a humorous anecdote about something that happened on the way through town—and, just for effect, another miracle at the end of the message might not be a bad idea.

Or consider the other side. Close your eyes for a moment and envision yourself part of the multitude. Why are you here? Maybe Jesus has changed your life through a miraculous act of healing. He has touched you so powerfully and personally that you want to be with Him as much as possible. What do you hope to hear from the Miracle Worker as He opens His mouth to speak?

Maybe Jesus has not affected you personally, but His teaching intrigues you. You believe there is more to life than the world offers, and what Jesus teaches about heaven rings true to your restless spirit. You want to hear more about this kingdom that He claims is inside a person rather than outside in the world. You can't do anything about the world, but you sure would like something to happen in your own life. You are here for the hope He stirs in your heart. What do you long to receive from the great Teacher?

Or, to be honest, you are not so spiritually minded. You are simply lonely and hope to connect with others. This looks like a place where that can happen.

You might be here out of curiosity more than anything else. You heard that Jesus provided food once for a huge crowd of thousands, and your deepest hope is that if you hang around long enough, something interesting will happen. You have no real expectations as the great man opens His mouth to speak, but, even so, you lean forward with interest. Others similarly look to Him, and the almost party-like atmosphere settles into an expectant hush. Pay close attention, because whatever your reason for being with the crowd, superficial or sincere, this is what you hear Jesus say:

"If anyone comes to me and does not hate his father and mother, his wife and children, his brothers and sisters—yes, even his own life—he cannot be my disciple."

Your feet shift uneasily at this strange beginning.

"And anyone who does not carry his cross and follow me cannot be my disciple."

You glance quickly to the left and the right to see if people beside you look as uncomfortable as you're beginning to feel. Why, of all things, does He use a death image like a cross?

Jesus is still speaking, so you lean forward once more and strain to catch His words. He mentions construction projects and wars, two endeavors not to be taken lightly. It is foolish to rush into either one, He says, unless you know what it will take to finish. Well, that makes sense, but what does it have to do with your life?

"In the same way . . ."

Jesus concludes with a sweeping statement. The bottom line is this:

". . . any of you who does not give up everything he has cannot be my disciple."

You sit back and let out a deep breath. The strong words ring in your ears.

> *"Anyone who does not carry his cross and follow me cannot be my disciple." Jesus' terms are all or nothing.*

"*Any of you . . .*"

Jesus leaves no doubt whom His words are for. They are all-inclusive. He means you as well as the person next to you and the one in front of you and ten rows behind.

". . . *who does not give up everything he has . . .*"

"Everything" is all encompassing. "Everything you have" is so . . . absolute.

". . . *cannot be my disciple.*"

"Cannot" is final. Jesus' terms are all or nothing.

I can imagine the uncomfortable silence that followed Christ's words. Those in the crowd who were paying attention had just heard some very hard statements. I can also see His closest disciples looking at each other with raised eyebrows. They had already heard a version of the "take up your cross" command at a time when Jesus' words were for their ears only (see Luke 9:23). Now He was making it clear that giving up everything to follow Him was not just for a select few. It was for anyone and everyone who wanted to be with Him. Surely some wouldn't accept this. Why would He make it so hard when things were going so well?

Jesus obviously did not play to the crowds. If these were His requirements for being a Christ follower, then He was not making it easy for them—or us, for that matter—to move out of the crowd and follow more seriously. Why? For two reasons: who He is and why He came.

Who *is* Jesus? More than a new face on the synagogue scene or a gifted teacher with radical ideas. More than the latest in a line of prophets calling people back to God. He is not just a rising star in a nation of restless people looking for healing or for a hero. Jesus is Eternity stepping into time,

Divinity mingling with humanity, God revealing Himself to His creation, the Son of God reclaiming what was lost.

And *why* did He come? Celebrity status on earth was not Jesus' dream. It certainly was not His reason for leaving eternity and stepping into time. The Son of God did not leave the Father's throne and all of heaven's glory to create an admiration society. He came to bring us back to the perfect relationship we had abandoned. He came to reclaim what was lost and restore what was broken. Such divinely ordained restoration happens only by Life on His terms—and His terms are clear:

> Absolute loyalty,
>> Absolute obedience,
>> Absolute surrender.

Something or Everything?

The question we must answer is this: *Will I follow Jesus on His terms?* Such a question hits close to home when His terms are so absolute. It reaches below a visible veneer of Christianity to hidden realities of the heart. It cuts to core beliefs and desires that reside deep within and will not leave without a fight.

Most of us, if we're honest, would agree with Alexander Moody Stuart's observation that "many are willing that Christ should be something, but few will consent that Christ should be everything." When I am most candid, I have to admit that this is often how I feel. Maybe not when I'm caught up in worship on Sunday morning—but on Monday morning when Jesus shines His flashlight on an area of my life that I am rather fond of, the struggle surfaces.

I saw the impact of this question on a student's face at Wake Forest University during my intern year with InterVarsity Christian Fellowship. Greg's initial response to the claims of Christ is probably an echo of what many in Jesus' day felt when He delivered His terms of discipleship.

He looked around with genuine dismay and asked, "Why does Jesus have to make it so hard?"

Greg considered himself a Christian when he entered his freshman year at Wake Forest, but like many in the crowds of Jesus' day, he was a distant follower. His first weeks of university life were occupied mainly with deciding which fraternity to join, but, in his enthusiasm for college life, he also investigated other groups on campus. As a result, Greg joined other students for a freshman retreat sponsored by InterVarsity.

In a sprawling old house in the beautiful setting of Montreat, North Carolina, IVCF staff and students ate, laughed and played together, and spent the morning and evening hours looking together at Jesus' terms of discipleship. Throughout Saturday afternoon Greg was right in the middle of the laughter and jokes, but as we studied the main Scripture passage that evening, I watched him become more and more quiet. In all honesty, I wondered if he was bored with such a serious focus after the day's fun. We were studying Jesus' words:

> Then he said to them all: "If anyone would come after me, he must deny himself and take up his cross daily and follow me. For whoever wants to save his life will lose it, but

whoever loses his life for me will save it. What good is it for a man to gain the whole world, and yet lose or forfeit his very self?" (Luke 9:23–25)

We divided into small groups for discussion after the teaching. Still quiet, Greg listened as others in his group shared their thoughts on the message. Finally, he lifted his head, looked around the group with genuine dismay on his face and asked, "Why does Jesus have to make it so hard?"

Greg was not bored. He had been listening and taking very seriously the demands of Jesus. He began to talk.

Before this weekend, Christ had meant something to him—but that "something" was little more than a belief and a standard of behavior that, admittedly, he might or might not follow depending on whom he was with at any given moment. Now he was confronted with a Christianity that called him beyond belief to a relationship of absolute surrender. How could he say no to what he knew was true? But how could he say yes to what would require everything of him?

As hard as it was to hear Jesus' terms of discipleship, Greg recognized truth, and he wanted to live by it. He yielded his life fully to Christ that weekend. The Spirit opened his heart and mind to the Life he was created to live, and it is not exaggerating to say that he became a new person. "New" is what happened when the real Greg met the real God (see 2 Cor. 5:17).

The old Greg was a soul disconnected from God, having a belief system of dubious influence over his life. The new Greg returned to campus a changed young man, not because he had renewed a commitment to his Christian beliefs, but because he had met Christ personally and was now His man above all.

Did this mean Greg never joined a fraternity? No, he was now following Jesus and learning from Him, and he saw that Jesus went where people needed Him. Greg caught on quickly to a truth about the Christian life expressed well by R.C. Sproul:

> We do not segment our lives, giving some time to God, some to our business or schooling, while keeping parts to ourselves. The idea is to live all of our lives in the presence of God, under the authority of God, and for the honor and glory of God. That is what the Christian life is all about.[1]

Greg's newness in Christ permeated every aspect of his life. He joined a fraternity and brought the presence of Christ with him.

Following from the Heart

If we hear Jesus' terms of discipleship without feeling uncomfortable, then we're probably not taking them seriously enough. But if His words challenge us to the core of our being—as they challenged Greg even after holding Christian beliefs for years—then we are hearing not only *what* God wants us to hear but *where* He wants us to hear it: not in our heads but deep in the heart.

The heart searches for God: "You will seek me and find me when you seek me with all your *heart*" (Jer. 29:13).

The heart shows what we truly value: "For where your treasure is, there your *heart* will be also" (Matt. 6:21).

The heart shows who we are from the inside out: "For

out of the overflow of the *heart* the mouth speaks" (Matt. 12:34).

Jesus' terms of discipleship are ultimately matters of the heart. Loyalty means I choose to love Jesus more than anyone else in my life, even those closest to me. Obedience means I choose to live a crucified life, even when I have to put to death impulses of my own heart. Surrender means refusing to set my heart on anything less than what God has eternally planned for me. These qualities are outward expressions of heart decisions.

How could someone yield so much? Not because of an ideal, but because of a Person.

We will look at these terms of discipleship as matters of the heart more closely in a later chapter, but we are faced with a heart choice even now. Jesus' terms of discipleship have not changed throughout the centuries. You and I are part of the crowd, listening and responding in one way or another. Do I respond by following more fully, or do I turn away because He asks too much?

Who Does He Think He Is?

A few questions may come to mind when you hear Jesus' terms, and they are legitimate. If someone is going to demand everything I have (and not at gunpoint but by my own free will), then I want to know who I'm yielding to so absolutely. Who is He to ask so much? What right does someone have to set such absolute terms of engagement?

C.T. Studd was the Michael Jordan of cricket in late nineteenth-century England. He was the son of a wealthy, retired planter who had made his fortune in India and then returned to England to spend it.

C.T.'s father was invited one night to hear the famous American preacher D.L. Moody. That evening, he gave his life unreservedly to Christ and then kept after his sons to do the same. C.T. and his brothers surrendered to Christ soon after, and each one followed Him as the Spirit directed. The famous young cricketer was led to give away his inheritance, nearly £30,000,[2] and spend his life serving Christ as a missionary in China, India and then Africa.

This popular and wealthy athlete gave up everything the world offered to be wholly available for Christ. How could he yield so much? Not because of an ideal he was trying to live up to, but because of a Person he knew and loved and found worthy to follow to the ends of the earth. His motto was, "If Jesus Christ be God and died for me, then no sacrifice can be too great for me to make for Him."

I am not suggesting that following Christ on His terms automatically means giving up money and possessions or even denying enjoyment of good things that God has given. Authentic spirituality is not a matter of external substance but of internal reality. It does not mean having only inexpensive objects in your home or choosing a missions trip for the yearly vacation rather than a week in Paris. If that were the case, then spirituality could be measured by outward conduct rather than the condition of the heart. We would be back to the very thing Jesus was working against in His day. The true measure of discipleship is being a Christ follower, bearing His image just as intentionally while vacationing in Paris as when serving in Calcutta.

How and where Jesus asks each disciple to live is up to

Him. Absolute loyalty of the heart, absolute obedience from the heart and absolute surrender of the heart are the marks of Christ followers, whether on the edge of the Sahara or in Chicago, whether building dispensaries in remote villages or serving with integrity in a downtown office.

Surrender Begins at the Cross

"You can't get second things by putting them first—you can get second things only by putting first things first," wrote C.S. Lewis. The first thing for a Christian is always the cross.

At the cross I face my sin that mars God's image in me and separates me from Him. I face the death I deserve, and I see that Someone has taken my place. At the cross I realize that I do not need another philosopher or another religion or another creed to tell me how to live. I need a Savior to break the stronghold of sin in my life and set my God-designed image free. Only God Himself could rescue me from what I am without Him. Rescue me He did, and at great cost to Himself.

Oswald Chambers wrote, "The centre of salvation is the Cross of Jesus, and the reason it is so easy to obtain salvation is because it cost God so much. The Cross is the point where God and sinful man merge with a crash and the way to life is opened—but the crash is on the heart of God."[3]

Love that pursued me through space and time, grace that forgave me, and a death that saved me. I kneel at the foot of the cross and receive undeserved mercy.

But meeting Christ at the cross and receiving forgiveness and freedom from sin is only the beginning. I stand up again and am never the same, because if I take Christ's death and my salvation seriously, another life must now die on the cross.

My image-projecting self-life—with all its dominating clinging cousins that make me self-centered, self-protecting, self-pitying, self-doubting, self-analyzing, self-seeking—faces its own cross when I accept Jesus' terms of discipleship. Nailed, dead and buried, never to be raised again. Good riddance! "Therefore, if anyone is in Christ, he is a new creation; the old has gone, the new has come!" (2 Cor. 5:17). Yes!

Heart Beats

The heart that listens:

> When we are called to follow Christ, we are summoned to an exclusive attachment to His person. . . . Christianity without the living Christ is inevitably Christianity without discipleship, and Christianity without discipleship is always Christianity without Christ. (*Dietrich Bonhoeffer*)[4]

Read Jesus' words in Luke 14:25–35 as though He was saying them to you now. Respond to Him, telling Him first how you feel when He asks so much of you, and then writing it in the form of a prayer. The following questions may help:

- Am I part of a "crowd" that meets because of Jesus (church, youth group, campus organization, Bible study)? If so, why?

- How would I identify myself at this time?

    ✧ A follower of Jesus
    ✧ A believer in Jesus but not a follower
    ✧ A seeker, still trying to discover what is true
    ✧ A spectator, participating more for the group than for personal change

- What is my relationship with Jesus when I'm not with the group or in church?
- Is Jesus "something" to me—or "everything"?

If you have read the Gospels all the way through, you know that very few from the crowds who followed Jesus were still with Him at the cross.

Read John 6:60–69 (it might be helpful to read verses 25–59 for the context).

- What choice did some of Jesus' disciples make after this teaching?
- What did Jesus ask those closest to Him?
- What was Peter's response to His question?

Following Jesus at this point was becoming less popular and more risky. It meant identification with Him when others turned away. How is this true for Christ followers today? Why should anyone stay with Jesus when others are refusing to follow?

A heart that responds:

Will I follow Jesus on His terms? Or will I remain in the crowd at a distance, following only as long as He has something to offer but turning back when He demands too much?

-3-

Treasuring

The owner of pearls pays no attention to shells. (*Francis de Sales*)

For where your treasure is, there your heart will be also.
(*Matthew 6:21*)

*F*aki Brahim and his family lived in a mud-brick and thatch hut one minute's walk down the dusty street from our house in Adré. His body showed the ravaging effects of leprosy, a disease which we tend to associate with stories from the Gospels but which is still prevalent in some countries today. Years of the disease's assault on Brahim's body had left little of his hands and feet. They were really nothing more than stumps.

We first met Brahim and his family when Louis began to treat his young son who was crippled from polio. The two men soon became close friends. Louis would walk to their meager home and sit with Brahim on a tattered plastic mat drinking small glasses of hot, sweet tea which the family could little afford—but which was essential to Chadian hospitality. Brahim would also come to our house and sit on our mat drinking tea with Louis.

One afternoon Brahim hobbled into our yard with his arms extended, clasping tightly between fingerless palms an upside-down, scrawny, live chicken. He approached Louis with a smile on his face, held out the chicken and said, "*Chilah, achan ana nehibbak, rafigi.*" Tears sprang to Louis's eyes, but not because of the gift; the chicken was small, and we could easily have bought another at the market. What touched Louis's heart were Brahim's words: "Take it, because I love you, my friend."

"Take it, because I love you, my friend." Brahim's attitude made all the difference.

Louis understood the sacrifice the gift represented. The chicken, lean as it was, could have provided a meal for Brahim's family or given them income. Our friend was surrendering something valuable; no one would have faulted him for keeping it.

Louis did not receive it lightly. In fact, he would have preferred not to accept the offering dangling upside down in front of him. But he knew that a refusal would have dishonored his friend.

The manner of Brahim's giving was precious. He was handing something valuable to Louis with genuine delight; his motive was to honor the relationship. That attitude made all the difference in receiving the gift.

Louis reflected later on his friend's posture. What if Brahim had brought the chicken in a different manner? What if he had approached Louis with his head low, mouth set in determination, feet dragging, and held out the chicken with the words, "I don't really want to do this, but I feel I have to. If I don't give you something, you might not keep helping my son. Here, hope you enjoy it."

How would Louis have felt? A motive of "have to" rather than "want to." Obligation over delight. He would have felt dishonored. His heart would have been saddened at the older man's efforts to earn his help and friendship. Any pleasure Louis might have received from the gift would have been diminished by the attitude of the giver's heart.

Two ways of giving. Same gift, but different motives. One attitude values the relationship and is joyful in giving, even at personal cost. The other devalues the relationship by giving from a grudging heart.

Honesty compels me to admit that at times I approach God in the second way. Service comes not with a smile but with a reluctant heart. Bible study and prayer are completed with the thought of ticking another item off my "to do" list for the day rather than in anticipation of time spent with God. Jesus' terms of discipleship are accepted with half-hearted acquiescence rather than joyful surrender. My focus is on what I am giving up instead of what I will gain.

Is it Sunday already? Guess I have to get up and get ready for church. I would love to sleep late just one morning of the week.

Do we have to tithe this much? By the time I give the government and God what they want, I have little left for myself.

Do I really have to give my boyfriend up? I know he's not a Christian, but I'm tired of waiting and trusting.

Do I really have to stop thinking this way, Lord? I mean, it's so hard to change, and no one will ever know.

Do I have to spend time with this person? She's so hard to be around, Lord!

You're asking me to go to Bulgaria? Can't I serve You just as effectively here?

Can you relate to any of these questions? No one would express them openly—it would ruin our Christian image! But God hears them and sees the heart attitude, even if others do not.

As Christians, we know God deserves our love and respect, and we know He will bless our lives if we obey Him. We also understand that He has a right to our time, money, personal desires and possessions, not to mention the right to rule our lives. But when God asks something of us which conflicts with personal desire—such as giving up a television show that flagrantly dishonors His standards—our response is very telling. When something is taken from us, our response reveals how much we value it.

God is not looking for a "have to" relationship with us. He looks for a "want to" relationship motivated by desire.

A friend suggested that such an attitude toward God is like a husband who says to his wife on New Year's Eve, "I'm a busy man and I have a lot to do, but I know I need to be more intentional about our relationship. So this year I'm going to set aside time in my schedule so we can have more time together."

The husband sits back, satisfied with himself at this generous resolution despite what it will cost him. The wife blinks, wondering what he really means. She may be glad at his decision, because it will undoubtedly mean some kind of improvement. But she will feel devalued by such an approach.

His words sound as if he is fulfilling a duty, not pursuing a desire. With such an attitude behind the offering, his wife's mind will be riddled with questions whenever the couple spends time together. *Is he physically with me but mentally at the office? Is he listening to me or thinking about a project? Does he* want *to be with me, or does he feel he* has *to?*

God is not looking for a "have to" relationship with us, one that colors our spiritual lives with dull hues of obligation and duty. He looks for a "want to" relationship in which service and obedience are motivated by desire.

Louis would have felt devalued if his friend had brought his gift with a grudging attitude. And God is devalued when we serve Him with dragging feet and reluctant hearts. Such service for Christ says, in essence, "I really don't want to do this, God, but I know I'm supposed to—so here, hope You enjoy it."

Hidden Treasure

Jesus told a parable of the Kingdom that speaks about heart attitude. It is a short story contained in a single verse, but its message is powerful largely because of one descriptive phrase: ". . . in his joy" (Matt. 13:44).

In the parable, a man discovered a treasure hidden in a field and wanted to obtain it. So he reburied the treasure, returned home and proceeded to sell everything he owned in order to buy the field.

That treasure must have been an incredible find for the man to do what he did. Everything in his life had to go for him to get enough money to buy it.

Using a bit of sanctified imagination, one can envision the scene that ensued when his wife came home from selling vegetables in the market. All her pots and pans, the bed, the furniture, the rugs—even the house itself—had been sold in order to buy a field she had never seen.

"That treasure," she mutters, "had better be worth it."

The man has seen the treasure. He knows its value.

"It is," he says. "Oh, believe me, it is."

She looks at her husband and notices his face. He has just sold everything. He has nothing now but a field and a treasure, yet his face is radiant with joy.

"In his joy," Jesus says, "[the man] went and sold all he had and bought that field" (Matt. 13:44). There was no half-hearted commitment or grudging acceptance. There was only joy in what he had found.

The key to this parable is in the man's heart attitude. The field cost him dearly. It cost him everything. But his heart rejoiced, because he valued what he gained far more than what he lost.

Worth the Cost

We show how much we value something by what we are willing to pay for it. If I see a pair of shoes that interests me, I usually turn one over to check the price. If the cost makes me raise my eyebrows, I set the item down quickly and move on. In my eyes, a pair of shoes, no matter how great looking or high-quality, is not worth what some stores ask.

On the other hand, when our daughter Elisabeth gave us one of her paintings a few years ago, I spent a considerable amount of time looking at custom frames to find just the right way to display her art. I have to admit that I walked out of the frame shop an hour later rather dazed, thinking, *I can't believe I just spent that.*

But whenever I see her oil painting on our wall enhanced by the perfect choice of frame and matting, I am not thinking at all of what I spent that day. The total look, not to mention the value we place on Elisabeth's art, is worth every bit they asked me to pay.

Value determines cost. No one argues when diamonds cost more than glass beads. First class service commands a higher fee than routine maintenance does. Pearls cost more than shells. We weigh cost against gain in making our decisions.

On a memorable afternoon in the fall of his senior year in college, I was talking with our son, Scott, about one of life's great questions: How do you know when you have met "the one"? He was thinking of Sarah, a young woman he had met at the University of North Carolina and had been dating for several years.

We knew Sarah and thought she was wonderful. We had also observed their relationship during the past year and believed it was a mature one. We could see that it was based on mutual commitment to Christ and a desire to honor Him on a secular university campus where anything goes. That was a good foundation, in our minds, for a life of faithfulness to Christ and to each other.

So here I was, talking with Scott about the possibility of Sarah as a permanent fixture in his life. As a mother, I was thrilled to realize we were talking about the "little girl out there somewhere" I had been praying for ever since Scott was a little boy crawling around in diapers. As a woman and wife, however, I wanted to make sure that my son knew the seriousness of this decision.

Marriage, for Sarah's sake and for his, was not to be considered lightly. Was he ready for it? As a journalism major with a focus in public relations, his promising contacts for the future would not be affected by marrying after graduation.

But going back overseas was also an option. Scott had expressed a dream of returning to Chad and helping the country of his childhood. Marriage would definitely put this dream on hold, at least for the immediate future.

"What do you want most of all?" I finally asked.

Without hesitation he said, "I want life with Sarah."

Scott's answer was confident and sincere, so I knew he meant it. Not a hesitant "I guess I have to give it up for now if I want to get married," but a matter-of-fact statement: "I've found something that I want more." Sarah was his greater yes that made other choices, however desirable, pale in comparison.

> *How much do we treasure Christ? Do we value Him enough to say, "I want You more than anything else"?*

As I write these words, Scott and Sarah have just celebrated their third year of marriage, and we are more delighted than ever to have her in the family. I no longer need to pray for my son's future wife. My new prayer is that they will remain each other's greater yes throughout life; that the inevitable challenges and potential pains of marriage will always pale in comparison to the gain of life together.

Jesus tells us in the parable that the kingdom of God is like a treasure hidden in a field. The man who discovered the treasure had no regrets in giving up everything for it. How much do we treasure Christ? Do we value Him enough to say, "I want *You*, Lord, more than anything else I might have apart from you"? Is Jesus the great Yes that puts all others in perspective?

Jesus' terms of discipleship are clear: Kingdom living requires not just *something* from us, but *everything*. To gain the full treasure, we must enter the Kingdom all the way. Halfhearted entering produces halfhearted joy and halfhearted obedience. Wholehearted entering leads to fullness of joy, obedience motivated by desire and a peace rooted so deeply in Christ that it remains, even through the deepest pain.

Treasuring Leads to Joy

Babies cry for milk when it is all they know. They struggle against the weaning process because they think there is nothing better than milk.

Why is that woman insisting I give this up? they might think. They have no idea what lies ahead. Applesauce, pureed peaches and mashed carrots; later on peanut butter and jelly sandwiches, corn on the cob, chicken cordon bleu and chocolate cake. If they knew, there would be no "have to" about weaning. There would be pure, expectant joy.

The man in the parable sold everything not because he had to, but because he wanted to; that is the point Jesus wanted to make. The man could not have bought the field for anything less. It cost everything, so he sold everything, but he sold it with joy, because his eyes were on the treasure. No matter what he had said yes to before that point in life, he had now found a greater yes. All other claims in life were measured against it and found wanting.

Jesus wants us to know that anything in life, no matter how valid and good, pales in comparison to life with Him. Having found Him, we have the best thing, and our hearts are filled with joy.

But of course this joy does not make sense to a world in which life must look a certain way—comfort, never discomfort; success, never failure; affirmation, never criticism; health, never illness; smooth skin and never wrinkles—in order for people to be happy. We can certainly enjoy good things, but our gladness does not depend on them. The Christian's joy is rooted in something deeper than surface realities:

> Though you have not seen him, you love him; and even though you do not see him now, you believe in him and are filled with an inexpressible and glorious joy, for you are receiving the goal of your faith, the salvation of your souls. (1 Peter 1:8–9)

Our joy, as Peter writes, is grounded in a Person. We are filled with inexpressible and glorious joy simply by loving and believing in Jesus. Heaven anticipated this joy and could not help but burst into song when God became a Man in the person of Christ. Joy featured in the announcement of Jesus' birth. "Do not be afraid," the angel said to the shepherds that night, "I bring you good news of great joy that will be for all the people" (Luke 2:10).

Joy comes from Jesus. "I have told you this so that *my joy may be in you* and that your joy may be complete" (John 15:11).

Joy comes from being with Jesus. "Now is your time of grief," He told the disciples before the cross, "but I will see you again and you will rejoice, and no one will take away your joy" (John 16:22).

"Rejoice in the Lord always. I will say it again . . . !" Paul counsels in a letter to the Philippian church. Why? Because "the Lord is near" (Phil. 4:4–5).

Paul's letter to the Philippians is filled with references to joy in Christ. Reading this letter is all the more challenging when we remember that it was written while Paul was in prison. Following Christ cost Paul his freedom and his reputation, but his eyes are on something else when writing the following words:

> But whatever was to my profit I now consider loss for the sake of Christ. What is more, I consider everything a loss compared to the surpassing greatness of knowing Christ Jesus my Lord, for whose sake I have lost all things. I consider them rubbish, that I may gain Christ and be found in him. (Phil. 3:7–9)

If Paul were a businessman, he might draw up two columns in his ledger. On the left he might list profit gained from his life before Christ, and on the right what he had gained with Christ.

The left column contains things the world would say yes to. It makes an impressive résumé for a man moving up in the religious world of Paul's day. His list includes a good heritage, an upstanding family, favorable connections, membership in the most powerful religious party of his day and right behavior—essential qualifications in the eyes of those he hoped to impress.

But in the other column, we see four words: *Christ Jesus my Lord.*

Everything left of the line now pales in comparison. Paul could have written the lines to a worship song I heard on the radio this week, "Everything is a lesser thing compared to You, Jesus." Before Christ, other things had value to Paul— and they were good things—but the real Treasure has put them in perspective.

When Paul looks at the left column and runs his eye over the advantages that had seemed so important, he no longer sees a list of good things that no one would fault him for pursuing, but a list ready for the trash can. Rubbish. Not even worth preserving. "One thing I do," he writes, "Forgetting what is behind and straining toward what is ahead, I press on toward the goal to win the prize for which God has called me heavenward in Christ Jesus" (Phil. 3:13–14).

> *Before Christ, other things had value to Paul—but a greater Yes has put them in perspective.*

Does Paul feel obligated to put on a happy face in very difficult circumstances because it is the Christian way to act? No, he *is* joyful because he sees something greater than his circumstances. His eyes are on Christ and not on the cost. Moving from the left column to the right is not loss but gain when Christ is our possession. Forgetting what is behind and pressing on toward what lies ahead makes sense when what lies ahead is valued above all else. For Paul, even in prison, there is no halfhearted sigh over what he has to endure—only wholehearted joy in knowing Christ.

Weighing the Cost

C.S. Lewis wrote a poem to his wife, Joy, when she was dying from cancer. *As the Ruin Falls* is vintage Lewis in its honesty ("I have never had a selfless thought since I was born") and hauntingly beautiful in its recognition that even in pain there is gain. Lewis tells his wife that she has helped him become the man he should be, but that the bridge she was building in his heart is now crumbling with her death. Though the poem is meant for Lewis's wife, my heart turns to Christ as I read its final words:

> For this, I bless you as the ruin falls. The pains
> You give me are far greater than all other gains.[1]

Life with Joy dying of cancer was painful, but Lewis would not have given up the pain for anything, because to be without the pain would have meant to be without Joy. Weighing cost versus gain, Lewis treasured life with her more than life without pain.

Can we say these words to Christ? "I treasure You, Lord, more than a pain-free life. I value You more than comfort, more than success, more than my carefully laid plans. I bless You in this painful circumstance because life with You, no matter how hard, is greater and more welcome than any life I might have without You."

These are sobering declarations. It certainly was not low-cost for God to restore us to life, and life with Christ is not low-cost if we are serious about living for Him.

Can I accept a costly gift from Christ, as C.S. Lewis had to do, and still rejoice? I can if my eyes are fixed on the One who has asked me to bear it.

Nothing between the Bare Heart and Jesus

Lilias Trotter was a young woman in her thirties when she first arrived in the deserts of Algeria. The year was 1888, and she had traveled from England by train and ship to serve as a missionary. She remained in Algeria for over thirty-eight years, serving the Lord she loved among the Muslim peoples He had put on her heart. Out of her ministry came the lasting legacy of a mission agency, the Algeria Missions Band (now Arab World Ministries).

Can I accept a costly gift from Christ and still rejoice?

Lilias left behind another legacy—a body of devotional literature written throughout her years in the desert land she chose to live in. Many of her writings include beautiful sketches illustrating truths she sought to express. The drawings are exquisite in detail and brilliant in depth, making one want to gaze deeply to take in every line and shade.

Such a reaction to her illustrations is not surprising. When the train pulled away from England's Waterloo Station, Lilias was leaving behind the very real possibility of a career as a brilliant artist. She had such talent that at age twenty-three she came to the attention of a man who happened to be the most famous art critic in Victorian England.

John Ruskin, artist and social philosopher, was one of the most influential men of his day when Lilias and her mother met him during a vacation in Venice. He was so enamored by her artistic skill that she became not only his student but a close friend.

At one point Ruskin told Lilias that if she would give herself to art, she "would be the greatest living painter and do things that would be Immortal." Such words were not to be taken lightly from a man whose opinion could make or break a career.

And Lilias did not take his assessment casually. She too loved art. But she could not give herself to it in the way Ruskin envisioned. It could not become the focus of her life. She had given her heart to a greater passion and focus, and she would soon follow Him into the desert. Throughout the remainder of her life, art would be a source of joy and creative expression, but it always remained a lesser passion, a lesser yes leaving room in her heart for the great Yes that is Christ.

Years later Lilias wrote the following words in a devotional entitled *Focussed: A Story and a Song*:

It is easy to find out whether our lives are focused, and if so, where the focus lies. Where do our thoughts settle when consciousness comes back in the morning? Where do they swing back when the pressure is off during the day? Does this test not give the clue? Then dare to have it out with God—and after all, that is the shortest way. Dare to bare your whole life and being before Him, and ask Him to show you whether or not all is focused on Christ and His glory. Dare to face the fact that unfocused good and useful as it may seem, it will prove to have failed its purpose. How do we bring things to a focus in the world of optics? Not by looking at the things to be dropped, but by looking at the one point that is to be brought out.

Turn your soul's vision to Jesus, and look and look at Him and a strange dimness will come over all that is apart from

Him, and the divine "attrait" by which God's saints are made, even in this 20th century, will lay hold of you. For "He is worthy" to have all there is to be had in the heart that He has died to win.[2]

He Is Worthy

One question runs like a thread through our twenty years as missionaries, usually coming to us after we have shared about life and ministry in Chad. While admiring the sacrifices we were willing to make in order to help people in such a poor country, someone inevitably wonders if such sacrifice is necessary.

Was it worth giving up a faculty position at the medical school? Was it worth bringing up our children in such a primitive place? Was it worth laboring year after year for only a handful of believers? Was it worth separating as a family while the children were in boarding school?

I have to admit that I have also asked this question at various points when the cost of obedience seemed especially high.

As we prepared to return to Chad after our first home leave, life on the left side of the Atlantic looked pretty good now that I had experienced life on the right side. Having already lived two and a half years in Chad, I knew what was waiting for us when we returned for another three. Sand and heat, charcoal fires, pit toilets and bucket showers, poverty at our doorstep and a fairly nonstop fishbowl-like existence.

A few days before we were to board the plane for our return, I sat on the back steps of the house where we were staying and said, "Lord, I'm going back only because I love You and want to be where You want me to be."

Once we returned to Chad, memories of life in America faded, and life in Chad took over. I settled again into the rhythms of this other country I was learning to love. It was not long before I was laughing again with Fatime, Izze and Achta, relishing the challenge of preparing meals in a doll-size oven and praying in earnest for our neighbors. I was, after all, glad to be back.

But here is the point. What enabled me to return when I did not feel like going back, when I was feeling instead the cost of obedience? Not an obligation

What enabled me to return when I was feeling the cost of obedience? Not an obligation, but a desire to love and honor Christ.

but a relationship. Not dutiful execution of a call but desire to love and honor a Person by my acceptance of His will. My desire to say yes to life in America was real, and I felt it; and it was not a bad thing to say yes to. But there was a Treasure to be gained that made everything else pale in comparison.

Louis and I have felt the cost of following Christ at different times during our years in Chad: cost to comfort, health, physical and emotional strength, being far away from family and friends. But we felt the cost of obedience most keenly as we neared the end of our second term of service when our three children, now approaching their teens, needed more education than we could provide in a remote African bush town.

We knew that our work in Chad was not yet finished. God had made that clear despite my giving Him ample time and opportunity to tell me otherwise. If Scott, Susan and

Elisabeth were to have the education we desired for them while we continued in Chad, the only option was boarding school. We made the difficult decision to let them go, and for the next six years they attended Black Forest Academy in Germany, four years for Scott before entering college in the States and six for Susan and Elisabeth until they graduated.

They thrived at Black Forest Academy, and God continually showed His faithfulness in the gift of such a great place for them to study, but it was a costly gift He had placed in our hands. Saying goodbye so often to my three greatest earthly treasures and not being fully part of their lives for months at a time was the hardest thing God had ever asked me to do. He must have heard me say more than once during those years, "I wouldn't do this for anyone but You, Lord. No one else is worthy of such a sacrifice."

"Is it worth it?" The hardship, the pain of separation, the sacrifice? Is it worth saying no to something I might have in order to say yes to something else Christ has for me —even though the gain may not be seen in the visible circumstances of life?

Louis and I have decided that when we hear this again, our response should be, "Actually, that's not the right question to ask." When measured against the value of knowing, loving and serving Christ, there is a more appropriate question. "Is He worthy?" The answer to that question is always "He is. Oh, believe me, He is."

Heart Beats

True love withholds nothing from Christ, when it is sincerely set upon him. If we actually love him, he will have our time, use of all our resources, and gifts, and graces:

indeed, then he shall have our possessions, freedom, and our very lives, whenever he calls for them. (*Thomas Doolittle*)[3]

The heart that listens:

Read the following accounts of people who interacted with Jesus. What dominates the life of each one at their point of interaction? What is the bottom-line "one thing" He says they each need?

Luke 10:38–42
Luke 18:18–30

John 3:22–30 records an account of another person who knew Jesus. His cousin, whom we know as John the Baptist, had a thriving ministry before Jesus came on the scene. What was bothering John's disciples (3:22–26)? Several things in John's answer reflect the greater Yes in his heart; what are they (3:27–30)?

The heart that responds:

In your journal make a list of things that matter most to you now—possessions, people, dreams, TV shows, a job promotion, a thinner body . . . Go through the list and, for each item, ask the question: If God said to me, "You can have this, but it will mean you cannot have Me," what would you choose? Your response reveals what you treasure.

Mentally place each item at the foot of the cross and back away, leaving it with Christ.

Some items on the list may simply need to be moved from first place to second in your life. Other items may need to be removed completely because you cannot honor Christ while keeping them in your life. Write in your journal what steps you will take to make Christ your treasured choice.

Remember that we are not yet what we should be, and God knows it. We can rest in His unconditional love and grace while pursuing life for His glory.

-4-

Emptying

Ask Him to fill your heart with all he would see in it.
(*François Fénelon*)

I pray . . . that you may be filled to the measure of
all the fullness of God. (*Ephesians 3:19*)

*D*uring one furlough in America, our family went to a camping store. After three years of bathing from a bucket, we were on the hunt for a shower bag, one we could fill with water and hook on a ceiling beam. When you live for long stretches of time without conveniences, simple pleasures—such as water pouring over the body from a bag rather than from a cup in your hand—begin to mean a great deal.

A store attendant saw the five of us and approached with a smile, probably thinking, *Ah, a family camping trip.*

"So, how long will you be camping?" he asked.

We glanced at each other and then turned to him. "Oh, about three years."

The look on his face was priceless.

We definitely did live a camping lifestyle in Chad. Although it was not always easy to live in such primitive conditions for long periods of time, we were committed to it, because a simple way of life was necessary in order to reach the people God had called us to serve.

For our first six years in Chad we lived in Adré, a bush town with no electricity or running water. Any light glowing inside the house came from a combination of kerosene and solar lamps. The water we consumed was brought daily in leather bags on the back of a donkey.

Living in a desert climate, one does not want to run out of water. We stored our supply in heavy plastic barrels stationed outside the kitchen door. These barrels were refilled daily, even if water remained from the day before.

Although refilling the barrels regularly was good for our daily supply, it was not good for the barrels, as we learned over time. The water came from local wells—and it also came with local dirt particles. We knew this, of course, and filtered what was used for drinking. But for household cleaning, bathing and cooking, the clear water drawn from the top of the barrel looked good enough to use. Focusing on the top of the barrel kept us from noticing what was accumulating at the bottom.

The *seyd al moya* (water master) was usually a teenage boy with the unenviable job of walking for hours in searing heat while beating a donkey with a stick to keep the poor animal going. His income depended on how many trips he made to the well, so he was no doubt glad to have us as clients. Sometimes, especially if we had guests, he would trek to the well and back on our behalf several times a day. Each time he returned to our house he poured and sloshed water from the leather bags via a noticeably unwashed plastic container, which no doubt added to our barrels' dirt multiplication.

One day we were chatting with the *seyd al moya* while he was making the transfer. We watched as the new water mixed with the old and stirred up what had been lurking below. We noticed the swirling particles and thought, *Hmmmm* . . . But they soon resettled at the bottom, and the surface appeared clean and clear again, so we let it go. The unhealthy particles were once more "out of sight, out of mind."

Soon enough, however, what was hidden within could no longer be ignored. After several months of mixing the new with the old, the bottom of the barrel became

What was hidden within could no longer be ignored. A vessel can produce only what it contains.

so dirty that even rinsing with fresh water would not wash away the darkening streaks of grime. We could no longer think that all was well just because things looked fine on the surface.

Clearly, something needed to be done. So we emptied the barrels completely, washed them meticulously and left them to dry in the sun. Then we started with a new load of water. From this point on, we regularly emptied our barrels of murky leftovers to keep the dregs from building up.

What Lies Within

Natural and spiritual principles are pictured in our dirty barrels. A vessel can produce only what it contains. Old and murky water at the bottom contaminates the new and purer water that goes in. For a container to purely hold something new, it must be emptied completely of what was in it.

The gap between life with God as it should be and the surface spirituality rampant in Israel in Jesus' day bothered Jesus so much that He challenged the spiritual leaders of His day in a way that did little to increase His popularity.

He saw image projecting rather than image bearing and spoke bluntly: "Woe to you, teachers of the law and Pharisees, you hypocrites! You clean the outside of the cup and dish, but inside they are full of greed and self-indulgence. Blind Pharisee! First clean the inside of the cup and dish, and then the outside also will be clean" (Matt. 23:25–26).

His words seem harsh to our ears, trained to political correctness of speech, but Jesus saw vessels created to contain the fullness of God (see Eph. 3:19) that were full of greed and self-indulgence. Fullness of God was replaced by fullness of self. His words were harsh, but His heart was breaking over how far His people had departed from their created identity and purpose.

Even today there are some who approach the Christian life as we approached our barrels and, in doing so, maintain the mindset of the Pharisees. Things on the surface look good enough, so it is easy to ignore what lies beneath. Spiritual life is measured by doing things Christians are supposed to do—attending church, being involved in activities, tithing, studying the Bible, praying. But this does nothing about the contamination that is still very much within us. We have added new behaviors, but in reality we remain just as we were before our life with Christ.

Surface spirituality produces hypocrisy in the church—the very thing Jesus condemned in the spiritual leaders of His day. Husbands and wives who are faithful church members have adulterous affairs. A church elder's wife discovers pornographic links on his computer. An abortion doctor is shot rather than prayed for. Homosexuals are pushed from new life in Christ by condemnation rather than drawn to Him by what they see in His followers. The women's ministry director refuses to talk to the pastor's wife. Gossip, slander and unwillingness to forgive tear a church apart. The list goes on.

None of us are perfectly what we should be. It is well said that if we are looking for a perfect church or a perfect mission, it will become *im*perfect the minute we step through its doors. But the sad truth is still all too real. There is sometimes very little of Christ in the church or in church members who bear His name.

Outward Christian behavior without inward change may as well be called "churchianity." Surface spirituality produces churchgoers but does not guarantee Christ followers. It skims the surface of life but does not reach to the core of our being and make us new.

I don't know about you, but this does not satisfy my soul. Something tells me that there is more than club membership and behavior modification to the Christian life. I long for a change so complete that when my life is shaken (as it will inevitably be), what rises to the surface is the character of Christ because so much of Christ is there.

Scripture makes it clear that this is God's longing for us, as well. His Word speaks about total renewal. There is the hope held out that we can actually *become* like Christ, not just act like Him.

Listen to what God says in His Word:

Therefore, *if anyone is in Christ, he is a new creation*; the old has gone, the new has come! (2 Cor. 5:17)

And we, who with unveiled faces all reflect the Lord's glory, are being *transformed into his likeness* with ever-increasing glory. (2 Cor. 3:18)

The amazing thing is that this is a personal goal of God for our lives from before we were born:

For those God foreknew he also *predestined to be conformed to the likeness of his Son*. (Rom. 8:29)

God's commitment to you and me reaches beyond changed behavior patterns. It involves more than *doing* what Jesus would do. His goal is that we think as Jesus thinks, so that what we do flows out of who we are. When we become like Christ, we live in the world as He would live.

In reality—and here is the glorious truth—God's intent is not that we try to live for Him as best we can. His intent is to fill us with Himself so that *He lives His life through us*. In exchange for what is inside us, contaminated since the Fall, He gives His life and all the fullness, freedom and glory that come with it (see Gal. 2:20, Col. 1:27). Life with a capital L.

This is deep stuff. And like the saga of our barrels, it needs more than a surface job to make us clean. The exchanged life begins on the inside. We must be emptied of all that would get in the way of what God has for us in Christ.

What gets in the way of the Christ life?

It is the self-life that lurks within: self-focus, self-will, self-love, self-consciousness, self-deceit, self-doubt, self-pity, self-righteousness, self-effort, self-indulgence, self-defensiveness, self-promotion . . .

When you think about it, there is nothing in this list we should be desperate to keep in the barrel.

"There is no smaller package than a person all wrapped up in himself," observed Peter C. Moore. My heart can say good riddance to self and its numerous clinging cousins and a resounding yes to William Temple's words: "The only way to deliver me from my self-centeredness is by winning my entire heart's devotion, the total allegiance of my will to God." Jesus' call for absolute obedience to my Creator makes sense when I understand that surrendering self is the only way to be freed from the binding of such a small package.

Jesus' call for absolute obedience is the only way to be freed from bondage to self.

We, like the people in the crowds who heard Jesus' terms of discipleship and like the Pharisees who heard His challenges, are vessels designed to contain the fullness of God. But we cannot fully contain His life until we are emptied of our own.

When we cleaned out our water vessels in Adré, we had to reach to the bottom of the barrels. In the same way, to deal completely with the contaminating particles of self, we must reach deep down to the bottom of our hearts. We must expose the pollution that influences how we think and what we love.

What's It All About?

First we must expose a matter of the *mind*—our contaminated worldview that causes us to think selfishly about God and ourselves. The first step in freeing our souls from self-focus is to replace it with God focus.

Louis was flipping through an airline magazine on a transAtlantic flight and noticed an advertisement for vacations at an island resort. Streaming across an enticing photo of serenity in the midst of luxurious comfort was the question, "Shouldn't the world revolve around you?"

I am not opposed to resort vacations—in fact, I would not mind one when this book is finished. But that question turns me off right away. I have heard it before, in the Genesis account of what was whispered into Eve's ear.

Satan's desire was to gain his own foothold in God's creation, and he sought to do this in the newly created souls God had placed in charge of the world. They were designed to think of themselves in connection with their Creator, so he needed to change the way they thought.

Their core belief that the world revolved around God and that His creatures function best as a reflection of His glory would not do for his ends. Satan gained his foothold when Adam and Eve bought the lie that the world revolved around the creature, not the Creator, and traded God's will for self-will. The results were disastrous—and self-will has infected the world ever since.

A worldview is our perception of what life is fundamentally about. It shapes how we interpret and interact with those around us. A self-focused perspective as blatantly advertised in the in-flight magazine comes from a deep belief that life is about us and our needs.

With a mindset like this, no wonder there is escalating frustration, anger and depression in the world. We think the world revolves around us, but unfortunately, no one else does. It has been well said that others are not thinking about us as much as we think they are—they are, more likely, thinking about themselves.

As Christians we would emphatically deny such a self-centered model of life, but this kind of thinking gains a foothold in the church when ritual replaces relationship and surface living replaces inner renewal. A Christianized version of a selfish worldview states that we have needs, and that these needs are met by Jesus alone. But it is easy to corrupt the transformational power of this truth by subtly twisting which needs we expect Him to meet.

Has Jesus died and been raised from the dead to give me a smooth, trouble-free life? If I think He died to make my circumstances better, then my will matters more than His, and what I want in life matters more than what He wants to do in my life. My will is naturally bent toward having a good life in which all my desires are fulfilled and all my needs met. With this bottom-line view of the world, Jesus is stuck in the middle of an equation that begins and ends with me.

The Bible makes it clear that the world does not begin and end with me but with God and His glory. The first words of Scripture are "In the beginning God . . ." (Gen. 1:1)—and we are not in the picture. Among the closing words in the final book of the Bible, the risen Christ says, "I am the Alpha and the Omega, the First and the Last, the Beginning and the End" (Rev. 22:13).

No matter what happens in the world—economic disaster or prosperity, war or peace, countries uniting or dividing, rulers rising or falling, freedom or persecution for Christ followers—God is at work. And one day "the earth will be filled with the knowledge of the glory of the LORD, as the waters cover the sea" (Hab. 2:14). He is fulfilling His purpose and, despite what we see with our physical eyes, the world is moving toward one goal "to be put into effect when the times will have reached their fulfillment—to bring all things in heaven and on earth together under one head, even Christ" (Eph. 1:10).

Returning to a biblical worldview from a distorted one is foundational in restoring our souls to their God-created image.

I am the one who fits in the middle of the equation and finds my place in God's will—not the other way around. This was the truth that revolutionized my life during the Young Life retreat and moved me from a Christianity in which I was the star of my own show, with Christ as acting coach, to one that put Christ on center stage as Lord.

Years later I would read the following words by Max Lucado which expressed this truth in his wonderfully down-to-earth style: "When God looks at the center of the universe, he doesn't look at you. When heaven's stagehands direct the spotlight toward the star of the show, I need no sunglasses. No light falls on me."[1] Absolutely.

Returning to a biblical worldview from a distorted one is foundational in restoring our souls to their God-created image. Satan's hold on our lives is broken each time we reverse Adam and Eve's initial self-decision and choose to take our proper place in the universe.

We Become Like What We Love

A second step in restoration of the soul is a matter of the *heart*: ridding ourselves of a displaced love.

Ralph Waldo Emerson, an American philosopher and poet, wrote, "The gods we worship write their names on our faces, be sure of that. And a man will worship something—have no doubt about that, either. He may think that his tribute is paid in secret in the dark recesses of his heart—but it will out. That which dominates will determine his life and character. Therefore, it behooves us to be careful what we worship, for what we are worshipping we are becoming."[2]

Emerson was not writing to Christians, but his words merit reflection. I cannot become like Christ while worshiping myself.

This brings us back to Jesus' terms of discipleship and helps us understand another reason they are so absolute. He knows that just as important as a change in what I *think* is a change in what I *love*. His wisdom and His love compel Him to require total surrender of that which keeps us imprisoned in the tight package of self. He commands absolute loyalty, obedience and surrender not only because He has the right to do so as God; He also knows that the way to love ourselves less is to love someone else more.

Richard Rolle, one of England's great spiritual leaders in the fourteenth century, put it this way: "People become like what they love; for they take their tone from the greed of their day and age. Because they will not give up their old ways, they come to prefer life's spacious emptiness to the warmth of happiness."[3]

Rolle's words were spoken in another era, but they are just as true today. We become like what we love. If we love the spirit of the age, it will fill our lives, and we will reflect that spirit through our actions, thoughts, reactions and words. If we love Jesus, then He will fill our lives, and we will reflect Him more and more.

Weighing the options, reflecting Jesus rather than the self-obsessed spirit of this age comes out on top in my mind. We only need to hear and see the Jesus of the Gospels to realize what a great thing this would be. When we empty ourselves of every thought and desire that is not of God, then Jesus has all the room He needs to fill us with Himself.

But how does this work on a practical level? How do I cooperate with the Spirit's transforming work of emptying and filling in the occupied minutes of daily life? Amy Carmichael received the following practical advice from a nineteenth-century British equivalent of Billy Graham, which she passed on to friends:

> Dr. F.B. Meyer once told me that when he was young he was very irritable, and an old man told him that he had found relief from this very thing by looking up the moment he felt it coming, and saying "Thy sweetness, Lord." By telling this, that old man helped Dr. Meyer, and he told it to tens of thousands. I pass it on to you because I have found it a certain and a quick way of escape. Take the opposite of your temptation and look up inwardly, name that opposite: Untruth—Thy truth, Lord: Unkindness— Thy kindness, Lord; Impatience—Thy patience, Lord; Selfishness—Thy unselfishness, Lord; Roughness—Thy

gentleness, Lord; Discourtesy—Thy courtesy, Lord; Resentment, inward heat, fuss—Thy sweetness, Lord, Thy calmness, Thy peacefulness.

I think that no one who tries this very simple plan will ever give it up. (It takes for granted, of course, that all is yielded—the "I" dethroned.) Will all to whom it is new please try it for a day, a week, a month, and test it.[4]

The habit of "looking up" inwardly while being occupied outwardly is one of the most practical ways to bring spiritual renewal into the business of our lives. An upward look of the heart maintains connection with God and can be done in a split second while carrying on a conversation or managing a business meeting.

Begin the habit of going immediately to God when you become aware of sinful attitudes, thoughts and habits. While looking in a mirror, entering a room for a meeting, beginning a project or talking with someone in the office—the moment a prideful, self-focused or judgmental thought occurs, take it silently to God.

Lord, I'm sorry for my critical spirit. Fill me with Your grace right now. Or, *I'm sorry for being so full of myself. Fill me with Your humility right now.* Then go on with the task at hand, trusting in the Spirit's transforming power.

The truth is that we are already filled with the life of Christ. Through being emptied of self, we merely give Him room to be Himself in us and to reveal Himself through us to the world. This echoes the words of Evan Roberts, an early 1900s Welsh revivalist: "When you go to the window, you do not go to look at the glass, but through it at the scenery beyond. Then look through me and see the Lord."[5]

Weighing Loss versus Gain

When Jesus spoke to the crowds, He spoke in terms of the heart (absolute loyalty) and the will (absolute obedience and surrender). Only deep transformation of core beliefs rooted in the heart and mind can produce change in our actions and reactions.

Only deep transformation of core beliefs rooted in the heart and mind can produce change in our actions and reactions.

Choosing God focus over self-focus can be scary, it is true, because we like to have control of our lives. I have heard many sincere Christians admit they are afraid to give their lives completely over to God, because they fear what He will ask them to do. Fénelon challenges these hesitations by reminding us that restoration is not about what we will do, but who we will become:

> What are you afraid of? Of leaving that which will soon leave you? What are you afraid of? Of following too much goodness, finding a too-loving God; of being drawn by an attraction which is stronger than self or the charms of this poor world? What are you afraid of? Of becoming too humble, too detached, too pure, too true, too reasonable, too grateful to your Father which is in heaven? I pray you, be afraid of nothing so much as of this false fear—this foolish, worldly wisdom which hesitates between God and self, between vice and virtue, between gratitude and in-gratitude, between life and death.[6]

What do I lose by admitting that the world does not revolve around me but around God and His glory? I lose the damaging effects of self-focus that keep me from becoming my true self. I lose the wrapping that keeps me imprisoned in a very small package.

And what do I gain?

Besides what I read in Fénelon's challenge, I gain God's Word to anchor my soul, His perspective to make sense of my circumstances, His strength to enable my work and His Spirit to renew my image. I gain a focus on God with all its glorious results: rest in His love, security in His care, fulfillment in His service and, most glorious of all, restoration of a lifelong companionship with the One who knows me most and loves me best.

I belong to You, Lord. You gave Your life so that I might have eternal life and that I might have Your life in me now. But I have not really lived my life for you. Even as a Christian, I confess that my life is more about me than about You. There is so much of "self" in this vessel, Lord, and so little of You. Make me a cleansed, pure vessel ready to receive all that You have for me —all of Your life in exchange for my own.

Heart Beats

We are in a strait place, indeed, when we are enclosed in self. But when we emerge from that prison, and enter into the immensity of God and the liberty of His children, we are set at large. (*François Fénelon*)[7]

The heart that listens:

Read the following verses. Reflect on whether or not you have made room for Christ in your life:

Luke 9:23–25

- How does Jesus' command express the principle of emptying and refilling?
- How would my life change if God takes possession of the inner springs of my being?
- Am I willing for this if giving God full control means changing the way I think and act? how I use my money? how I relate to my family? how I handle my business? which television shows and movies I watch? which books I read?

The heart that responds:

Recognition

Ask God to reveal particles of self-life that lurk within. Pay attention to reactions, thoughts and leanings of the heart in the coming weeks. The Holy Spirit will use them to reveal pride, a critical spirit, a complaining spirit, laziness, selfishness, impurity, greed, prejudice, resentment . . .

Instead of being discouraged by what you see, thank God for loving you too much to let it remain in your life. Remember that God is not surprised by what lies within. He understands sin and is ready to forgive, heal and restore. He does not mean us to dwell on our imperfections but to deal with them.

Release and Receive

Along with developing the habit of short prayers during the day, get alone with God for a more concentrated time of dealing with the sinful attitudes He reveals. Release each one through confession and repentance, and then receive Christ life in its place.

Self-centeredness is replaced by God centeredness, resentment by forgiveness, criticism and judgmental tendency with grace, indifference with compassion, complaining with thankfulness, impurity with purity, materialism with simplicity and generosity. You might pray in the following way:

Lord, I repent of my concern over the opinions of others that drives what I do and keeps me wrapped up in myself. I release its control on my life. Fill me with a concern for Your glory and honor above all.

Lord, I repent of pride that keeps me focused on myself and affects how I relate to and view others. I release its control on my life. Fill me with Your humility and Your focus on others. Help me to walk into a room saying "There you are" rather than "Here I am."[8]

Entering

It is only with the heart that one can see rightly; what is essential is invisible to the eye. (*Antoine de Saint-Exupéry*)

The reality, however, is found in Christ. (*Colossians 2:17*)

*D*esert places are good for reality checks. At least this is the opinion of Paul Shepard, a renowned ecological philosopher and writer of the last century. "In the desert go prophets and hermits," he wrote. "Through deserts go pilgrims and exiles. Here the leaders of the great religions have sought the therapeutic and spiritual battles of retreat, not to escape but to find reality."[1] Shepard was not writing from a Christian point of view, but he is right about finding reality in desert places. Left with yourself and a stark landscape, you quickly find what you can and cannot do to survive on your own.

During our years in Chad we lived very much like the Chadian people themselves. If we had mourned the loss of comforts and conveniences left behind in America, we would not have survived.

We did not want to mourn them, though. An affinity for camping helped, but we arrived in Chad with a mindset of embracing the life and culture God was calling us to as missionaries.

So we lived as a family of five without electricity and running water, replacing these conveniences with solar lamps and bucket showers under the stars. We sweated inside mosquito nets on lumpy cotton-stuffed mattresses when temperatures soared at night, skimped on water when the rainy season was late in coming, cleared away sand, grit and dust blown in by winds from the north and read to our children at night by flashlight or kerosene lamp.

Holding the current book of choice in my hand, I would sit on the cool cement floor at the intersection of the children's rooms so my voice would carry through the open doors as Scott lay listening in his bed and Susan and Elisabeth in theirs. For these nightly readings, I learned to prefer the flashlight, because it held less attraction for kamikaze beetles and moths.

If Louis had mourned the loss of medical conveniences left behind at the University of South Carolina where he had taught in the residency program, he would certainly not have survived as a physician. The district hospital where he now served had no electricity or running water. His office was a small, almost claustrophobic room with pockmarked walls and a rusty metal desk and cabinets for furniture. When he arrived in Adré to assume responsibility of the district's health care, there was no pharmacy to ensure a ready supply of medicines, and the operating room still had bloodstained cloths lying on the floor from the last operation performed years before.

Louis worked hard to develop the health care system of an extremely impoverished government district. This meant improving the small, thirty-bed hospital so that a father riding his camel into town with a feverish child in his arms could finally get the chloroquine needed for malaria. It also meant motivating villagers to build their own clinics from mud brick and wood overlaid with cement, and training nurses for these clinics so the same father would never again have to travel two days for basic health care.

Spiritual challenges produce great desert experiences.

Letting go of physical props in his profession meant Louis had to boil surgical instruments over a fire in our backyard until he could improve conditions enough to do sterilizing procedures at the hospital. It meant finishing an operation by flashlight when the hospital generator broke down in the middle of a C-section. And it meant dancing a jig when a shoebox arrived, sent by a physician friend from home, that contained just the medicine he needed to treat one of his patients. Stripped of what seems necessary, you learn what is possible with what you have in hand and with a great deal of prayer.

Spiritual challenges produce equally great desert experiences. The Western church takes for granted devotional books, Bible studies, prayer meetings, worship CDs, fellowship dinners and Sunday sermons that provide continual nourishment for the soul. But these are not always accessible in remote places of the earth. They may actually be nonexistent, especially when the dominant faith of a region is Islam.

Not long after I became a Christian, someone challenged me with the words, "I used to think that God was important in my life, until I learned that He is enough." These words came to mind over and over again during our years in Chad. Left with ourselves and God, we find out fairly quickly what we need to survive spiritually. We learn whether our walk with God has depended on surface props or on a connection with God Himself.

I would add a note to Shepard's words: In the desert, whether it is physical, emotional or spiritual, I discover the true source of my strength. Does my life depend on outward props that may be taken away, or do I draw strength from within, from a relationship that can never be upset no matter where I am or what I experience in life?

Thriving in the Desert

I would often look at the stark landscape surrounding our town and wonder how anything could survive in such a harsh environment. Yet trees not only survived but thrived in the Sub-Sahara; many were lush, green fruit trees that yielded a seasonal abundance of mangoes and guavas for local markets.

Trees on the edge of the Sahara endure extreme conditions of wind and weather, yet they manage to stand tall, spread their branches and bear fruit. In an often bleak landscape which offers next to nothing for comfort, these trees provide shelter for birds, food for camels and shade for anyone who passes by. How do they manage to more than survive—not just hanging on for dear life in difficult circumstances, but giving of themselves to the world around them?

The answer is no secret, of course, to anyone who has studied botany or pulled a plant from the ground and exposed its roots. The active life that we observe above ground is anchored in another life below the surface.

A tree has two lives, as Evelyn Underhill, an Anglican poet and author in the early twentieth century, noted in her book *Concerning the Inner Life*. She wrote that a tree shows only part of itself to the world: It has a vast system of roots which are often greater and more extensive than the branches themselves. This buried source of life provides the strength and stability of the tree. Its durability is directly related to the depth of its unseen life.

Our Two Lives

People also have two lives which are directly related. Most obviously, we have an external, observable life. This life actively changes with passing seasons; it produces fruit, extends branches and makes, hopefully, a positive impact on those around us. And at some point, if we are living and breathing, it feels the crushing heat and harsh wind of circumstances that inevitably blow our way.

We also have a life seen by no one but God. This is the hidden life of the soul connecting with God through Christ, the eternal Source of life. It is born of a heart that leans toward Him and a mind established in His Word. Like a tree with its concealed system of roots, the strength of our visible life depends on the private life in our soul.

We tend, even as Christians, to focus on what can be seen, and we too easily ignore the true life of the heart. This is not new by any means. The pull toward outward impression has affected the church since its birth in the first century. Surface spirituality and club mentality have kept people busy in church life while distracting them from life in Christ. I am convinced this is one reason many people grow up attending church only to leave it as adults. Their relationship has been with a church rather than with the person of Christ.

> *Throughout the history of the church, there have been men and women who understood that the key to right living has ever been heart transformation through Christ.*

Thankfully, throughout the history of the church, there have been men and women who understood that the key to right living has ever been heart transformation through Christ. Depending on whether or not the church itself was connected to Christ at the time, these mystics and reformers have not always been appreciated for their efforts.

Madame Jeanne Guyon, from the seventeenth century, is one who was appreciated by many for the depth of her relationship with Christ—but not by church leaders. Madame Guyon wrote a small book that revolutionized the lives of many Christians in her day. It also landed her in the infamous Bastille prison in France, because her emphasis threatened the then-current trend of observable spiritual acts imposed by the church. In this influential book, originally titled *A Short and Very Easy Method of Prayer*, she wrote:

> The heart is all important if we are to go forward in Christ. Once the heart has been gained by God, everything else will eventually take care of itself. This is why He requires the heart above all else.[2]

Though the church was a powerful and influential force in her day, Guyon's simple book wielded a deeper and more lasting influence in the lives of many who read it. Feeling the gap in their spiritual lives, readers sought a deeper intimacy with God. Their hearts resonated with Guyon's reminder that true godliness grows from within:

> If godliness is not from deep within you, it is only a mask. The mere outward appearance of godliness is as changeable as a garment. But when godliness is produced in you from the Life that is deep within you—then that godliness is real, lasting, and the genuine essence of the Lord.[3]

The same hunger and thirst for a lasting and genuine spirituality is evident today. Many people in churches feel they wear a mask of godliness and long for something deeper.

Deserts tend to unmask us in sudden and unexpected ways by toppling the props we lean on. Health is stolen by an accident or illness. Financial security is removed through loss of a job. Friends are taken away through a transfer to another town. Marriage is destroyed through a divorce. Reputation is lost through slander. Comfort evaporates through a move to the edge of the Sahara. If we have not paid attention to our hidden life with Christ, these things easily uproot us and leave us lying dry in the desert, hardly knowing what hit us.

Evelyn Underhill suggests that focusing on external spirituality will produce a life tied to three verbs—to want, to have and to do:

We mostly spend those lives conjugating three verbs: to Want, to Have, and to Do. Craving, clutching, and fussing, on the material, political, social, emotional, intellectual—even on the religious—plane. We are kept in perpetual unrest: forgetting that none of these verbs has ultimate significance, except so far as they are transcended by and included in the fundamental verb, to Be: and that Being, not wanting, having, doing, is the essence of a spiritual life.[4]

Wanting, having, doing. Craving, clutching and fussing. Do these sound familiar? If they do not describe your life, they may bring to mind someone you know or even the church you attend. They certainly describe the general state of the world. When we forget (or acknowledge, yet ignore) our private life with Christ, nothing is left for us but a surface veneer with its unstable props and perpetual unrest.

"Being, not wanting, having, doing, is the essence of a spiritual life," suggested Underhill. "Being" denotes resting. If outward living results in perpetual unrest, then an inner life rooted in God will produce continual rest.

I have learned more about a hidden life with God from Moses than from anyone else in the Bible. Reading through Exodus, I see someone whose surface props were taken away as a young man. Forced to flee Egypt, he experienced incredible challenges in his years of leadership and management in the desert.

Yet I see also a man who grew steadily stronger in faith and leadership ability. I see Moses moving from self-focus to God focus and from fearful obedience to faithfulness in the midst of life challenges—and I wonder how he got there.

Ongoing Habit for the Challenges of Life

Recently I returned to Exodus for devotional reading and discovered something I had not paid attention to before, written in such a "by the way" manner that it was easy to overlook. In what seems little more than a parenthetical pause in the middle of the action, we discover a habit of Moses that fed his relationship with God.

It was this habit that kept him going through hard times and changed him from the self-focused, ineffective and fearful man we meet at the beginning of the book to the God-honoring one we see at the end.

Most of the events Moses lived through would break the stoutest of hearts and challenge the most gifted of leaders. There is no doubt from the text that Moses deeply felt the challenges that obedience to God threw his way. But he kept going, even through ministry pressures and setbacks, slap-in-the-face disappointments, criticism and open rebellion from the company he was called to lead.

Under these emotional, physical and spiritual demands, what kept Moses from throwing in the towel and returning to his former, simpler life as a shepherd in Midian (which he surely must have looked back on with longing from time to time)?

The "parenthetical pause," which we find in Exodus 33, contains the source of Moses' strength:

> Now Moses used to take a tent and pitch it outside the camp some distance away, calling it the "tent of meeting." Anyone inquiring of the LORD would go to the tent of meeting outside the camp. And whenever Moses went out to the tent, all the people rose and stood at the entrances to

their tents, watching Moses until he entered the tent. (Exod.
33:7–8)

At some point in the journey between Egypt and the
promised land of Canaan, Moses had developed a practice
of designating a place some distance from the camp for spending time alone with God. I can imagine that every time the
Israelites found a new location, one of the first things Moses
did was scan the horizon to see where he would put the tent
of meeting. Meeting with
God was so vital to his life
that the question was never
if he would get alone with
God, but *where.*

> *If we are serious about spiritual growth, we will be serious about spending time with God.*

Moses was able to
handle the challenges of
leading a vast and often re-
bellious nation because he
had developed a habit that anchored him in something unseen. A strongly rooted tree can weather any storm, because
it hasn't waited for the storm to break before reaching deeply
into the ground. And so it was for Moses. By the time the
crises hit, he was already connected deeply with God.

As Christians, we are taught that in order to grow in our
faith we must spend time alone with God. Whether this
practice is called a "quiet time" or "the morning watch" or
simply devotions, it is taught as a discipline of the Christian
life. If we are serious about spiritual growth, we will be serious about spending time with God.

The habit of "entering the tent" for Moses, however, was
not a discipline taught by spiritual mentors. At this point in

time, there were no regulations in place for life with God. The official tabernacle with its pattern for worship was not even in existence.

Meeting alone with God for Moses was not about personal growth. It was about relationship. As we read further into the description of this habit, born out of desire rather than duty, we can see why it became so vital to his life.

An Ongoing Conversation

The people who watched Moses regularly enter the tent could see no further than the flap closing behind him. What happened within was concealed from their eyes. But we have the privilege of seeing behind closed doors, so to speak. Like the proverbial fly on the wall, we witness what happens inside; and what we observe is a conversation taking place: "The LORD would speak to Moses face to face, as a man speaks with his friend" (Exod. 33:11).

Habitually spending time in God's presence touches on something deeper than formulas, such as designating times and places for devotions. It reaches below the surface to the way we relate to God.

One might expect a meeting between deity and humanity to be marked by formal protocol. But distance and formality do not form the scenario here. The interaction we witness is warm and personal, and it involves conversation as intimate as that between friends.

"Prayer is the expression of the human heart in conversation with God," wrote Rosalind Rinker. "The more natural the prayer, the more real He becomes. It has all been simplified for me to this extent: prayer is a dialogue between two persons who love each other."[5] We get the idea that such a conversation and such a relationship are developing between Moses and the Lord.

What intrigues me most about their interaction is who leans toward whom in friendship and who does the speaking.

We tend to have a one-sided approach to God, leaning heavily on our side. "For many of us it is true to say that our prayer life is far more preoccupied with who we are than who God is," suggests Mark Stibbe in *A Kingdom of Priests*. Prayer becomes a monologue rather than dialogue. We pour out our hearts; God listens and does something about what we tell Him.

Yet in this glimpse into Moses' life, we see that God is speaking, and Moses listens. I think Moses would have agreed with Gloria Gaither's assertion: "In our relationship with God there is much to be said, and God is the one who must say it." He learned early on that his ability to persevere through hard times had more to do with God's side of the conversation than his own.

The first chapters of Exodus make it clear that when God intends to do a great work, He does not guarantee smooth sailing or immediate results. Between God's promise of deliverance in chapter 3 and its fulfillment in chapter 12, there are false starts and crushing disappointments. But Moses' relationship with God can be seen developing through this process.

Chapter 4 ends with hope and worship: "Moses and Aaron brought together all the elders of the Israelites. . . . And when they heard that the LORD was concerned about them and had seen their misery, they bowed down and worshiped" (4:29, 31). *God is with us! He is going to help us!* Hope is high for the Israelites, and it is a good beginning for Moses.

Not long afterward, Moses and Aaron go to Pharaoh armed with God's instructions and promises. They say what God has told them to say—but what happens? Pharaoh not only refuses to listen, but he makes life more miserable for the Israelites than before. The Israelites in turn take out their anger on Moses. Chapter 5 ends with a thoroughly discouraged Moses.

So obedience has not brought results. Instead of deliverance for the slaves, their situation is worse. There is nothing obvious to encourage Moses, and he tells God exactly how he feels: "O Lord, why have you brought trouble upon this people? Is this why you sent me? Ever since I went to Pharaoh to speak in your name, he has brought trouble upon this people, and you have not rescued your people at all" (5:22–23).

God is more pleased with one raw heart than an entire service of eloquently executed but superficial prayers.

I love Moses' honesty with God; it reflects the depth of their relationship. Friends of the heart speak openly with each other without fear of rejection or censure. Moses tells it like it is, questions and complaints included. There are no dressed-up speeches, no rehearsed litanies; just the real Moses speaking with the real God.

His dilemma does not bother God. The Lord knows what Moses is feeling. I like the way Jeff Lucas puts it in his book, *Elijah: Anointed and Stressed*:

Be honest with God. Tell him what you really think. He knows your heart anyway. Sometimes I think that we pray our poetic, flowing stanzas and it is as if God says, "Oh, give me a break! Cut the long speech telling what you think I want to hear. Just tell me the way it is!" [6]

God is more pleased with one raw heart filled with questions and doubts brought honestly to Him than an entire service of eloquently executed but superficial prayers.

God does not want our *words*. He wants our *hearts*, raw or otherwise, and receives the words because prayer is how we talk to God. What we see Moses doing time and again throughout the ensuing chapters is returning to God. There are more setbacks and discouragements, but he keeps going, and he keeps dialoguing with God.

Moses' side of the conversation is open and honest. He tells God his frustrations and admits his doubts, and God speaks in return. Between the promise and its fulfillment, God tells Moses two things over and over again in His side of the conversation: He reminds Moses of who He is and what He will do.

While Moses listens, God speaks a continual "I am" and "I will" into each situation. Moses not only listens to God, but he takes Him at His word and draws strength from His character and His promises. He keeps going. He keeps obeying. He keeps trusting until the promise is fulfilled.

It is not a passive waiting and trusting. In listening to God, Moses is receiving guidance—both for dealing with Pharaoh and later in the desert crises he faces. He is also gaining an understanding of the character and promises of God.

The Lord speaks the same things to us today. I have walked with God for over thirty years since that night by the stream, and I have studied the Bible in one way or another nearly every day of those years. But more and more I view reading God's Word not as a spiritual discipline but as a conversation.

When I spend time with God, He speaks to me through His Word; I listen to what He says, and I respond in prayer. Then I talk with God about what is on my heart; He listens to what I say, and He responds through His Word. His answer may not come on that particular day, but at some point He tells me what I need to hear—if I am listening.

In every book of the Bible, God reveals Himself to His people in some way. Whether through history or prophecy, through books of the Law or poetic songs, God speaks about Himself, about us and about the world in which we live. He clarifies our circumstances and gives us guidance. Are we listening to God or merely reading a passage for the day?

Reading the Bible conversationally occurs when I read to know God better rather than to know the Bible better. I hear His voice speaking personally when Scripture relates to someone I am concerned about or something God wants me to think about. I respond by stopping to talk with Him about it. And so the dialogue continues.

A Changed Life

When we spend time with people, they influence us, whether we realize it or not. Similarly, the more time we relate to God personally, the more His likeness and character mark our lives.

This is what happened to Moses. The habit of spending time in God's presence transformed him.

I have to admit that it greatly encourages me to remember that Moses did not begin as a man of much faith—or of much use to God, for that matter. His first encounter with God was less than stellar and in fact reveals someone highly preoccupied with self. Their first conversation is strewn with "what if" hesitations and "I can't" declarations (see Exod. 3 and 4). Self-focus, self-doubt and self-protection exposed an obsessive concern about the opinion of others and a practically nonexistent desire to be used by God.

By the end of his life, however, Moses is a changed man. His focus has shifted from self to God. Preoccupation with his inadequacies has become trust in God's power—and God has used Moses mightily for His purposes.

One of Moses' last recorded conversations with God is found in Exodus 33. It occurs on the heels of the golden calf crisis and is a far cry from his first encounter with God. It reads like a dialogue between friends. Moses' heart has obviously become passionate for God's glory.

C.H. Spurgeon wrote, "In the deserts of affliction the presence of the Lord becomes everything to us, and we prize His company beyond any value." Moses found he could survive the challenges of life in the desert because of an ongoing conversation with God that rooted him firmly in a source of strength outside himself. The very real circumstances of life did not destroy him, because of a parallel reality in relationship with God.

It is no wonder that in the New Testament book of Hebrews, Moses makes it into the chapter 11 "hall of faith" because of all he accomplished for God. But in the middle of the impressive litany of his accomplishments, the writer

of Hebrews tells us the source of his strength: "He perse-
vered because he saw him who is invisible" (Heb. 11:27).

Heart Beats

God will teach you more than all the most experienced
persons or the most spiritual books can do. (*François
Fénelon*)

The heart that listens:

Meaningful conversations are not likely to happen where
noise and activity provide distractions. Conversation can go
only so deep in a crowd, even among friends. You begin to
long for a place where you can hear each other speak. The
tent was that kind of place for Moses. Once inside, he was
with God and away from the noise and clamor outside. He
and God could hear each other speak.

Jesus also had a habit of pulling away from people and
ministry in order to be alone with God. Read the following
verses, remembering that prayer was Christ's means of com-
municating with His Father. Note especially the record of
Jesus' habit in Luke 5:16.

Matthew 14:22–23   Luke 6:12
Mark 1:35   Luke 9:18, 28
Luke 5:15–16   Luke 11:1

The heart that responds:

- Have you "entered the tent" lately for personal time with God? If not, decide now on a time and place where you will regularly get alone with God for listening to Him through His Word and talking with Him through prayer.

- Practice reading your Bible as conversation with God. The Psalms are good for this, especially ones such as Psalm 16, 73 or 142. When a situation comes to mind as you read or a verse challenges you, stop and talk to God. Use the Scriptures before you to pray about it; then continue reading.

-6-

Remaining

One can have a very busy day, outwardly speaking,
and yet be steadily in the holy Presence. (*Thomas Kelly*)

So then, just as you received Christ Jesus as Lord,
continue to live in him. (*Colossians 2:6*)

*O*ur home in Chad often felt
like Grand Central Station—people coming and going at all
hours. Some days I felt closed in physically by the walls surrounding our yard, but even more confining was the emotional pressure from constant demands at the front door. I often longed for some, for any, physical and emotional space where I could retreat in order to restore perspective.

There were two doors to our house. At the front door centered all the activity. It was there we met the outside world, welcomed visitors, interacted with merchants and beggars, answered questions and responded to needs. Through it we also brought small glasses of strong, sweet tea to drink with friends. The open door signaled that we were available to anyone who came by.

The second door, directly opposite the front, led to a small, dirt-packed backyard. Activities outside this door included throwing out dishwater, hanging laundry on nylon ropes to dry, plucking chickens for lunch and setting up beds when it was too hot to sleep inside. Rarely did a visitor walk around the house to the back door.

One morning, in a desperate effort to have momentary relief from the demands of life at the front door, I exited the house through the back door, sat down on a rough stool made of wood and rope, and leaned against the house with eyes closed. For a few blissful minutes, I sat in quiet, feeling the warmth of a sun-baked house against my back and letting the welcome quiet soak into my mind.

When I opened my eyes again and looked straight ahead, I saw only a cement wall; but when I looked up, I saw the sky.

There were birds flying overhead. My eyes followed their unhurried movements on the warm currents of air, and my spirit wished I could sprout wings and fly with them, away from the demands waiting on the other side of the house. After a few moments of watching, my tangled emotions began to unwind, giving me emotional space to think again; and I talked with God.

I told Him what I was feeling—from the frustration of being little more than a pocketbook for those with yet another monetary request to the weariness of interacting with a constant stream of visitors. And, to top it off, there was guilt. I was a missionary. Missionaries are loving and patient, and that morning I was, most decidedly, not.

As I talked with God, bringing the real me into His presence and holding nothing back, frustration and guilt relaxed their clenching grip. Repentance pushed away my bad attitudes. Grace nudged away the guilt. A Father held his weary daughter. For that moment, I flew with the birds in the wide, open spaces, borne up by unseen currents of air, unhurried and free. And after awhile I was able to return to the other door renewed in strength.

Our back door reminds me of another one—a tent door in the desert through which the burdened leader of a massive nation was ushered into God's presence. Both Moses and I received strength in the quiet presence of God to meet the demands waiting on the other side of the door.

For Moses, the tent was not simply a momentary getaway from the maddening crowd—although I can well imagine that he let out a sigh of relief every time he closed the flap on the noise and clamor behind him. This habitual withdrawing provided, more than anything, the opportunity for a relationship to be formed.

Repentance pushed away my bad attitudes. Grace nudged away the guilt.

In the same way, my backyard was for me more than time out from the pressures of life. It provided time in God's presence. My strength was fast becoming depleted by the claims of a busy morning, but it was renewed through reconnection with my Source of strength.

This spontaneous time in God's presence happened more from desperation than design that morning, but because I went beyond sitting on a chair and soaking in the quiet to reconnecting with God, I rose with more than just a few minutes of outward peace and quiet in a busy day. I had a renewed relationship with God, and "doing" once more flowed out of "being." Ministry flowed once more from His strength, His perspective, His compassion and not from my own limited efforts.

There were other occasions after that day when I enjoyed a moment in the backyard, leaving the door of my public self and entering God's presence. But as with Moses, my purpose was to obtain a quiet goal of the heart: staying connected with God during the course of a busy day.

The wonderful truth is that we do not need a physical door, because the spiritual door of the heart is always open, and we can step through it any time of the day. We can stay continually in God's presence, remaining connected with Him even while talking with others. We do not need to pull visibly away to be secretly communing with God.

Time alone with God is essential to life with Him; it plays a major role in our transformation. We need to be with Him in private, so we can hear Him speak and have undistracted time for developing relationship.

But Moses knew as well as you and I do that God is not limited to specific places and times. He can show up in the flames of a burning bush. He can speak on a mountain, by rocks and springs, and give instructions in the middle of a crisis with the distracting background noise of an oncoming army.

Moses had enough experience with God to know that when he left the tent of meeting, he did not leave God behind, sitting alone like an old man waiting for his friend's next visit. Neither do we leave God sitting by our "quiet time" chair when we finish morning devotions and begin preparations for the day.

Our tendency is to relegate our relationship with God to specific times and places. We connect with Him in church, Bible studies, prayer meetings and in the time we set aside for personal devotions, as if God joins us in the spiritual parts of life and nothing else. This is our idea, not His.

"I'm staying with you," He says to us (see Heb. 13:5). The conversation we began with Him in our morning Bible reading and prayer continues as He goes with us out the front door and into the day.

Remain in Me

Staying connected is so essential to the Christian life that Jesus made sure His disciples understood its importance before He left them to return to the Father. He was not prone to repetition when teaching His followers, but in one conversation He repeated a phrase five times in nearly as many sentences: "Remain in Me."

The Passover meal was finished, and the disciples were on their way with Jesus to the Garden of Gethsemane. They had no clue as to what lay ahead, but Jesus was well aware that the world as they knew it was about to be turned upside down. Everything they had staked their lives on by being with Him would seem to fall apart. Christ would be arrested and then crucified, and they would face external hostilities and internal doubts.

That was just the immediate future. Beyond Jesus' resurrection and return to heaven, a church would burst into life with the coming of the Holy Spirit. The disciples would face enormous ministry responsibilities trying to manage a newly formed community of literally thousands of believers.

And opposition toward them would continue. Some of them would have to defend themselves in courts of law, some would be martyred and all would face persecution.

Jesus knew that the men with Him would be stretched emotionally, physically and spiritually in ways they could not anticipate. This was His last opportunity to speak with them before the cross, before life would "happen" and disrupt all their plans.

Principles of effective ministry are good tools, but Jesus gave something far more vital. He gave Himself.

What would you say before leaving your closest friends, knowing they will carry on your work? Would you outline key points of ministry development for the church they will soon have to manage? Would you give five steps to effective leadership? Tell them, "Memorize these points and do these things and you will be guaranteed success"?

Principles of effective ministry and leadership are good tools to have in hand, but Jesus gave none of these at this crucial time. He gave something far more vital for handling life and ministry challenges. He gave not a plan, not a method. He gave Himself.

As they headed toward the scene of His arrest and crucifixion, Jesus wanted the disciples to know that the end of His physical life was not the end of their life together.

You can almost see Him leaning toward them as they walked, His hand unconsciously pointing to Himself as He spoke. As you read what Jesus said to His disciples, hear Him speaking to you, and see Him leaning toward you— and know that He is giving the master key for handling the challenges you face:

> *Remain in me*, and *I will remain in you*. No branch can bear fruit by itself; it must remain in the vine. Neither can you bear fruit unless you *remain in me*.
>
> I am the vine; you are the branches. If a man *remains in me* and I in him, he will bear much fruit; apart from me you can do nothing. If anyone does not *remain in me*, he is like a branch that is thrown away and withers; such branches are picked up, thrown into the fire and burned. If you *remain in me* and *my words remain in you*, ask whatever you wish, and it will be given you. This is to my Father's glory, that you bear much fruit, showing yourselves to be my disciples.
>
> As the Father has loved me, so have I loved you. Now *remain in my love*. (John 15:4–9)

A thread of three words runs through His exhortation, words of command: "Remain in me. . . . Remain in me. . . . Remain in me." And a promise: "I will remain in you."

I can see our friend, Jim, who once spoke with Louis about the conclusive words in Hebrews 13:5, wondering again with a shake of his head, *What is it about God's commitment to stay with us that do we not understand?*

We know that prayer was not simply a spiritual discipline for Jesus but His vital connection with the Father. Jesus now tells the disciples, "Follow my example. Do what I did. While I was on earth, I remained connected to my Father. Now you stay connected to Me."

"Remain in me" is a command. But Jesus also gave the promise, "I will remain in you." The disciples had heard this before the cross, but not until after the resurrection did they understand how it was possible.

The cross was not the end of life for Jesus, nor was it the end of His presence in their lives. Rather than marking the end of connection with Jesus, the cross was the beginning of a more intimate relationship.

Before the resurrection, He could only be *with* them. Afterward, He could be *in* them. As they walked to the garden, Jesus taught them that through His resurrected life and the infilling of the Holy Spirit, they would have the life of the Vine itself flowing in them.

The key to spiritual life lies not with methods or programs or disciplines designed to help us grow, as helpful as these are—but with Christ. Without connection to the vine, there is no life for the branches.

We can be as busy as we like with spiritual activities and be faithful in maintaining spiritual disciplines, but without Christ's life, these behaviors merely skim the surface. They are more like artificial fruit fastened to a tree rather than what is naturally produced from a tree's inner life.

I have nothing deeper than surface spirituality to offer others if there is nothing deeper going on in me. I certainly have nothing of Christ to give to others if there is nothing of Christ in me.

Christ within is a reality for all Christians, but not all Christians live as if it was true. Charles Trumbull, in his classic, *Victory in Christ*, observed that while we say "I accept Christ into my life" we often go on to live as if we have said, "I accept the Christian life, and now I'm going to live it."

Scripture makes it clear that we are not taking up the Christian life; we are taking in Christ:

> Do you not realize that Christ Jesus is in you? (2 Cor. 13:5)
>
> I have been crucified with Christ and I no longer live, but Christ lives in me. (Gal. 2:20)
>
> To them God has chosen to make known among the Gentiles the glorious riches of this mystery, which is Christ in you, the hope of glory. (Col. 1:27)

Christ's life in us is the only way to have the Christ life flowing through us, remaking us, touching those around us. I find this incredibly freeing and hopeful. It frees me from self-effort and the false idea that I can make myself as good as I want to be, if I only try hard enough. It reminds me that the way to more Christlikeness is not more Susan trying to imitate

Christ's life in us is the only way to have the Christ life flowing through us, remaking us, touching those around us.

Christ, but less Susan, period. I get out of the way so Christ has room to be Himself in me and reveal Himself through me.

Instead of thinking, *I will love this person if it kills me*, I can freely, honestly and humbly admit, *I can't love this person, Lord. I don't have it in me apart from You to love as I should. But You* are *in me. Love through me, love of Christ.* And I, with my conditions and demands on others, get out of the way and let Christ love through me.

Instead of walking into a room with a mental *Here I am* with its typical self-consciousness, I get my concern about others' opinions out of the way by walking in with a mental *There you are*—giving Christ room to care for others through me.

I have hope that over time, as self gets out of the way and Christ has increasing room to be Himself in me, I will be changed. Christlikeness is more and more who I am, not how I am trying to behave. The *shem* of outward appearance is a true reflection of the *nepesh* of inward reality. Image projecting becomes image bearing once again.

This is all very well and good, you might think, *doing flowing from being, Christ living in and through me. But really, how does it work? Give me tools to go with the inspiration!*

I am with you there, and have often wished that God would just zap me and make it happen. He could, if He wanted, take a split second rather than a lifetime to restore us to His image. That would be so much easier for us and—it seems—much more glorifying to Him to have perfectly behaved Christians in the world.

But God did not create robots, much as I long for a quick road to transformation. He created human beings with hearts to desire, minds to think and wills to choose. Even with the very real presence of Christ in us and the Holy Spirit shaping us, God still treats us as the human beings we are.

God allows us to desire, think and choose, which means we still are able to do these things unwisely, even downright wrongly, as He watches.

But being an agent of free will means also that I have something of myself to offer God. This is a continual offering, since I am continually desiring, thinking and choosing throughout the day.

It also means that I keep relating to God, not out of mindless duty but out of conscious love. I have a part, then, in the transformation process. I choose daily to stay connected to Christ who is the image and fullness of God in me.

I cannot say it enough, because Jesus Himself repeated it. Apart from Christ we can do nothing. Only Christ, who is the exact representation of God, can restore that image in us. And only connection with a very real Christ in the deep places of our hearts can produce genuine Christ life in our practical lives.

We have an advantage over Moses. Because Christ lives in us, as Paul wrote to the Colossian church, we carry our "tent of meeting" everywhere we go. We remain connected in the heart and mind even when there is no time to pull away physically for a few minutes of quiet. At any time during the day, we are able to enter God's presence and keep the conversation going.

Keep Entering

Doors make up a big part of our lives, when you think about it. We open and close doors toward and away from activities and relationships all day long: doors to a conference room, a class, a store, a hospital, a friend's house, a restaurant, an office. As we're stepping through these multiple doors, the door of the soul remains open and keeps us rooted in one relationship.

Amy Carmichael's missionary calling to India at the end of the nineteenth century led to a lifelong ministry of rescuing children from sexual exploitation in Hindu temples. The Dohnavur Fellowship began out of Amy's work and grew into a large Christian community where she lived, surrounded by children and staff and frequent visitors until her death in 1951.

She writes from her experience as someone who was fully engaged with people:

> When you cannot any more shut your door, cannot count on being alone, it is easy to forget that there is another door which can be shut. We can sink deep into the quietness which is within and not without. . . . We can emerge (as it were) from that stillness at a word, at a touch, and yet remain within it. In Him, not in our circumstances, is our peace. As of old, so it is today.
>
> In Christ, in Colosse; in Christ, in hospital; in Christ, *here*.
>
> O Thou, who are more near to us than air,
> Let me not miss Thee, ever, anywhere.[1]

Staying connected with Christ begins with remembering He is more near to us than air. We do not have to think God into being. He is with us already, and not only with us, but in us.

While living at the front door of life—talking with others, tapping out emails, filing reports, discussing business, driving to the store, laughing with friends at a party or figuring out what to prepare for dinner—we are with Christ through the hidden door of our soul. We just have to remember and live what is already true.

This is not as easy as it sounds, of course. Since the Fall, we have been disconnected with God at this deeper level of the soul. We have forgotten who we are, souls created for belonging and connection, and so we have to relearn soul-level intimacy.

Soul connection happens as we remember each day that Christ is our closest companion. Intimacy is restored as we walk and talk with Him throughout the day, do everything with Him and bring everything to Him.

Over time, Christ becomes as real to us as our closest earthly friends, because, in truth, He *is* as real. Fénelon would say that we connect with Christ even more than with people, because "we can never be as real with our best earthly friends as fully as we could wish, but we can be so to any extent with God."

Over time, Christ becomes as real to us as our closest earthly friends, because, in truth, He is as real.

Think of points during your day that can trigger awareness of Christ's presence in you. This is not thinking Him into existence, but acknowledging that He is already with you and engaging Him in conversation.

Driving is a good time to carry on a conversation, so let entering the car be a signal to talk to God. Speak out loud if you are alone in the car and in the heart if others are with you. *Lord, help me to really care for Joan right now. Be with Sam at school today, Lord, especially in the math class that's so hard for him.* Develop the habit of getting in and out of the car with an attitude that says, *Going with You, Lord.*

A physical door can remind you of entering a building or room with Christ. Acknowledge that He goes in with you and that in Him you have all you need for what lies ahead. Whether a business meeting or a shopping trip awaits you on the other side, you are never alone. So go through praying, *Let's do this together, Lord.*

Apart from the companionship factor and the joy and peace this brings to us personally, it is also true that we bring the presence of Christ with us. Will others in the room see something of Christ during the meeting? Will they see His character in the way I interact with them? Will they be drawn to Him in some way because I have been in the room?

Scripture tells us that we are the fragrance of Christ (see 2 Cor. 2:14), and entering a room is a good time to ask, "Am I producing the aroma of Christ today?"

Entering a room with a "There you are" focus rather than a "Here I am" attitude enables us to cooperate with Christ in caring for people we meet. When we leave a room, we want the atmosphere of Christ to remain like a fragrance that lingers long after its source is gone.

Intentionally remembering Christ's presence during the day may seem difficult at first, and we may well groan at the thought of something else to consider in an already overloaded day. But again, because we are not used to keeping divine company, we must be purposeful about it at first. The outcome will be worth the effort.

This is not about becoming a more spiritual Christian by adding spiritual activity. It is about knowing and loving Christ more deeply, walking with Him as your closest companion and best friend—who happens also to be your Lord and King. Over time, awareness of Christ's presence becomes as natural as breathing. There will come a point when you no longer have to think about living in His presence, because you just do.

Keep Talking

How does one carry on a conversation with God when other things require concentration in the course of the day?

We have work to do, with our hands and with our minds. Paul exhorts the Thessalonians to "be joyful always; pray continually; give thanks in all circumstances, for this is God's will for you in Christ Jesus" (1 Thess. 5:16–18). How can we respond to God's command to pray continually, yet still get things done?

Praying continually is a problem only if I reduce prayer to the physical act of bowing my head and closing my eyes for a period of time. But there is a way to pray continually while carrying out our daily responsibilities.

In our practical work we do not strictly think about God all the time. We cannot, because we are thinking about other things. But we can bring God into our thoughts of other things.

People *think* constantly; so a very practical way to *pray* constantly is to turn our thoughts into prayers. This is probably the most practical and effective way I know of cultivating the companionship of Christ. Simply put, instead of merely thinking about something, say it to God.

I was feeling discouraged about this chapter as I wrote it. It did not come together easily, and I was feeling convinced there is no need for another book under the sun. And if there is, I am obviously not the one to write it.

So I tell God what I am thinking. Honestly, openly— the real me. Not a dressed up me wanting to impress Him with my faith in the face of discouragement. Discouraging thoughts, honest fears, become a conversation with the One who can do something about them.

Praying my thoughts develops in this case into more than conversation. It becomes transformation. Talking with God is better than brooding over imperfections; self-focus turns to God focus in the few seconds it takes to turn thoughts into prayer.

Turning thoughts into prayers is especially helpful if my thoughts are less than kind, which happens more often than I wish. It is well said that we can love anyone when we are alone. I can leave my house after a great quiet time with God, filled with loving thoughts for His world, and then see a neighbor who always seems to have a sour expression. Her countenance can destroy my joy more quickly than anything.

Criticism flares up. Judgmental thoughts rear their heads. Immediately, I turn them into a prayer of repentance. *I'm sorry, Lord. Forgive me for being judgmental.* Or a prayer of blessing: *Lord, bless her with good things today.* And I go on with my day. In a split second I am connected with Christ and changed within.

I remember one time I was aware of judging a friend. My first thought was, *I don't want John to know I'm thinking this way about him.* In other words, I felt I should cover up my attitude. On the positive side, I didn't want to hurt my friend's feelings. But on the negative side, I was trying to project a dishonest image of caring rather than judging.

Right on the heels of this was the Lord's counter thought. *No, you don't need to cover up what you think. You need to change how you think.*

I knew He was right. *Lord, forgive me for such a critical spirit. Help me to love, truly love and appreciate, John for who he is and for what You are doing in his life.*

"Do not conform any longer to the pattern of this world, but be transformed by the renewing of your mind" (Rom.

12:2). The world's thinking patterns shape our minds every day through media, conversations, advertisements and cultural trends. Ask the Holy Spirit to shape your mind by making you aware every time a prideful, self-serving, judgmental or impure thought comes to mind. If you are sincere, He will gladly raise your awareness of what needs to be changed.

Ask the Holy Spirit to shape your mind. He will gladly raise your awareness of what needs to be changed.

I can vouch for that. In the past I would not have thought twice about glancing at my reflection when passing a window. It seems a natural, almost a Pavlovian, response. But now the Spirit has reminded me that pride and self-focus are behind such a glance, as simple as it seems. And the thought, *Do I look okay?* becomes the prayer, *Lord, forgive me for being so concerned with appearances.* Or simply, *You, Lord; not me today.*

When I lift my mind to Christ, I am changed as I cut sinful thoughts short and move on with my day. Criticism is dealt with through a prayer of repentance or of blessing. Pride is cut short by whispered repentance. I shut the door on grumbling by praise and thanks.

The way I think is reshaped through continual conversation with God, and in turn, the way I interact with people and respond to circumstances is changed as well.

Turning our thoughts into prayers also cultivates companionship with the Lord. Bringing Christ into spontaneous moments takes only a second of time, and intimacy is deepened through sharing experiences together.

A beautiful sunset can be shared with Him: *Lord, it's so lovely!* We can have the same response to an evening of laughter and conversation with our children: *Lord, thank You for making this happen.* And during that family time, I can bring each one before the Lord, thanking Him for them and asking His blessing on their lives. I can take comfort in His presence when entering a room full of strangers: *OK, Lord, it's You and me together. Let's go meet some people.*

Frank Laubach writes, "Whisper to the Lord about each small matter." That does not take much time. The thought turned into a prayer can be as simple as the Jesus prayer, prayed since the days of the early church: "Lord, have mercy on me, a sinner." It can be thanking the Lord so much throughout the day that eventually the words spring from your lips without prior thought.

Throughout the history of the church, prayer as conversation with God has been taught by lay people and theologians. Clement of Alexandria said in the second century that "prayer is keeping company with God." Brother Lawrence, in the seventeenth century, wrote: "God is everywhere, in all places, and there is no spot where we cannot draw near to Him and hear Him speaking in our heart."

And Matthew Henry encouraged us to speak with Christ "as to a friend we have love and freedom with; such a friend we cannot go by without calling on, and never want [or lack] something to say to although we have no particular business with him; to such a friend we unbosom ourselves, we profess our love and esteem, and with pleasure communicate our thoughts."[2]

No matter what century or country brought us these mentors from the past, they all draw from the one spiritual key Jesus gave the disciples on His way to the cross: "Remain in me, and I will remain in you" (John 15:4).

Most of us have seen dances in which two partners become one fluid motion. They move in such harmony with each other that eventually they blend together as one. Remaining connected to Christ in the world reflects the Christian's dance. When we fellowship with Christ wherever we go, and when the Christ who lives in us is then seen by others, our hidden life and our visible life will move as one.

Keep entering His presence. Keep talking with the Lord throughout the day. As we remain in Christ, we will keep becoming all we are meant to be.

Heart Beats

The only reason He extended those arms on the cross was so He might embrace you. Tell me, what possible risk do you take in depending solely upon God? What risk do you run by abandoning yourself completely to Him? The Lord will not deceive you (that is, unless it is to bestow on you more abundance than you ever imagined).

However, those who expect all of these things from the Lord by self-effort will hear the Lord's rebuke: You have wearied yourselves in the multiplicity of your ways, and have not said, "Let us rest in peace." (*Madame Jeanne Guyon*)[3]

The heart that listens:

The following verses show that Jesus' prayer life extended beyond set "quiet times" with the Father to daily, moment-by-moment conversation, bringing God spontaneously into His daily life.

John 11:41–42
Matthew 11:25
Luke 9:16

The heart that responds:

Jesus looked up and talked spontaneously to God. We can "look up" in the heart at any time and talk with Him.

- What can I do to remember that Christ is with me wherever I go today?
- Ask the Holy Spirit to help keep the conversation going by turning thoughts into prayers in the coming weeks.

Think about the physical doors you enter and exit in the course of a day in light of the following questions:

- How can I remain with Christ in the activities that happen beyond the door?
- Who will I interact with on the other side of the door?
- How can I be the fragrance of Christ to them?

Seeing

Lift up thine eyes and see
As far as mortal may
Into Eternity;
and stay thy heart on Me.
(*Amy Carmichael*)

And Elisha prayed, "O Lord, open his eyes so he may see."
(*2 Kings 6:17*)

*H*ere on the sands just south of the Sahara, houses are still made of mud and thatch. Villagers farm with handmade tools and cook in heavy iron pots perched on three rocks framing a wood fire. Nothing indicates that one is actually in the twenty-first century. Coming from modern America, it made us feel immersed in a world time seems to have forgotten.

Louis visited these villages often in his role as medical director, and on every visit he felt as though he was traveling back in time. Not decades, but centuries. Men, women and children had never seen a television or a magazine to help them visualize a world outside the boundaries of their village.

One evening as he sat around a fire talking with a family, they heard the far-off sound of a commercial jet passing overhead. The irony of the moment was not lost on Louis.

In the plane was another world altogether: laptop computers, iPods, in-flight movies and heated dinners in small plastic trays. The people with Louis had no idea what that unseen world above them was like. Conversely, most people in the plane were totally unaware of the world in an isolated African village just thousands of feet below them.

Two worlds very near each other. Two realities happening simultaneously. Neither one can see the other, but both are real.

We live daily in two different, yet very real, worlds—one seen and the other unseen. Science and secular philosophies with such slogans as "seeing is believing" have lulled us into trusting only what we see with our physical eyes. But the Bible reminds us there is more to life:

> Now faith is being sure of what we hope for and certain of what we do not see. (Heb. 11:1)

> So we fix our eyes not on what is seen, but on what is unseen. For what is seen is temporary, but what is unseen is eternal. (2 Cor. 4:18)

According to the writer of Hebrews, hope and certainty are anchored in the eternal. This is good news, because what we see in the world does not look hopeful. God's Word, however, gives us great hope. The question is, will we respond to the world with our physical eyes only, or will we see and respond with the eyes of faith?

Open His Eyes

The prophet Elisha, like Moses, had a habit of the hidden life that spilled over into daily living. Moses talked with God as a close friend; but what marked Elisha's relationship with the Lord was that he viewed his circumstances by faith. He knew that our natural eyes are impaired, since the visible world exposes only half the picture.

The most vivid example of Elisha's spiritual sight is recorded in the Old Testament record of Israel's kings. The events leading up to the account read like a novel of modern espionage (2 Kings 6:8–23).

What marked Elisha's relationship with the Lord was that he viewed his circumstances by faith.

The nation of Aram was waging war against Israel. Aram's king would hold strategy sessions with his officers to decide where their troops would next set up camp in order to catch Israel's army off guard.

Every time they chose a new location, however, Elisha would send word to Israel's king and warn him, "Beware of passing that place, because the Arameans are going down there." The king of Israel would check it out and then step up his guard in that location, thus foiling the Arameans' plans.

This happened so often that Aram's king was sure there was a spy among his officers. In an understandable fury, he summoned them and demanded, "Will you tell me which of us is on the side of the king of Israel?"

One of his officers informed him that he had a bigger problem than a mere spy. "Elisha," they told him, "the prophet who is in Israel, tells the king of Israel the very words you speak in your bedroom."

Such information would put fear into any man's heart, but would especially shake a political leader. It is not surprising that the king put in motion an immediate plan for Elisha's capture. He discovered where the prophet lived and sent a "strong force" to capture him. They traveled through the night and by morning reached the city of Dothan where Elisha and his servant lived.

Early that morning, the servant stepped outside the house. I can imagine him shutting the door quietly, thinking sleepily, *It is way too early to go to the well for water*. As he turned around, he must have jerked back with such violent surprise that the clay jar in his arms crashed to the ground. What he saw terrified him. The city was surrounded by an army with horses and chariots.

The shock would be similar to having a perfectly normal day turned upside down by a call from your doctor: "Come in for a second exam as soon as you can. Today would be good." Nothing can make those words sound hopeful. And nothing about a huge army surrounding the town looked hopeful in Elisha's servant's eyes.

His first response was a cry of panic. "Oh, my master, what shall we do?"

Elisha thrust his head out the door, looked on the same scene and had a very different response. He spoke words of certainty and hope. "Don't be afraid," he said. "Those who are with us are more than those who are with them."

The servant might be forgiven for not feeling immediate

hope just because Elisha had spoken a few words of comfort. As far as his own eyes could see, there was no one on their side except the two of them and the inhabitants of a sleepy town. Not great odds against armed and mounted soldiers.

Elisha understood the seriousness of the situation. He knew the army had come for him. But he also knew something besides the physical reality was happening. There was more to this than met the eye: They were not alone.

But his servant did not yet know what he knew, so Elisha prayed. His words are an example for us when we are up against something that threatens to destroy us. Elisha did not pray for changed circumstances. Instead, he asked God to change the way his servant saw the situation: "O LORD, open his eyes so he may see."

God answered Elisha's prayer. "Then the LORD opened the servant's eyes, and he looked and saw the hills full of horses and chariots of fire all around Elisha." For an incredible moment, God opened the physical eyes of the servant to see the world of the supernatural.

It is important to realize that the horses and chariots of fire he was enabled to see were not a divine hologram projected on the hills for his encouragement. They were an army as real as the Arameans', and they had been there the entire time. The servant simply had not seen them.

Completing the Picture of Life in this World

Elisha's servant had been suffering from impaired vision. Until God opened his eyes, he saw only half the picture. In the same way, we have limited understanding of life on earth until we see with faith-filled eyes.

Sometimes God pulls back the curtain of heaven, and, like Elisha's servant, we are given a glimpse of heavenly realities. My friend Jean, while living on her own for several years, told me about a night in which she saw an angel in her hallway.

I believe her. Of all of my friends, she is probably the least given to spiritual excitement or flights of fancy. Neither am I. But even though I have never seen anything similar, I have at times sensed a spiritual presence. And I've heard enough stories from reliable people to believe that seeing angels is possible.

But God does not always give us natural glimpses into the supernatural world. Instead, He pulls back the curtain and reveals unseen realities through His Word and commands us to see them with eyes of faith.

God's point of view, revealed to us in Scripture, enables us to see the big picture.

When Louis and his Chadian friends heard the distant noise of the airplane overhead, he tried to explain what goes on inside, but they had difficulty imagining something they could not see.

He was wishing that he had with him a book from our shelf at home. The illustrated airplane descriptions would have added colorful and detailed images to his words, giving a visual glimpse into the "world" passing by thousands of feet above them. In that moment, the two worlds could have touched.

God has given us such an account that helps correct our impaired vision. The Bible is one long record of interaction between the seen and the unseen. God's point of view, revealed to us in Scripture, enables us to see the big picture of what is happening in the world.

From the first chapter to the last, the Bible makes something clear: The spiritual world, not the physical, is our lasting reality. As we have noted in an earlier chapter, the first words of the Bible are "In the beginning, God . . ."

The world did not exist before the creation, and the final chapters of Revelation reveal that it will also have an end. We will exist forever, but not in the framework of this world. God has plans that outlast what we hear on the evening news.

I was talking recently with a friend about her work in China. She shared that the past year had been extremely difficult because of what was happening in the lives of her Chinese friends. There were times when she felt close to despair at the crushing weight of their problems and difficulties. "All I know to do is to pray," she told me.

We talked about where we turn when we have no idea what to do, when we cannot "fix" life for ourselves or others—or, for that matter, the world. We go to Someone whom we see only with the eyes of faith.

We do not pray because prayer works. We pray because God works, and by faith we trust that He is indeed working from His side, completing the picture.

There is good reason to despair if our understanding of life is limited to what we read in the daily headlines. But Christians are not limited to news reports. We know that another reality is at work, governed by the hand of a loving and wise Father.

When someone asked Billy Graham if he was discouraged by what was happening in the world, he replied, "I've read the last page of the Bible. It's all going to turn out alright."

We do not let the world's half of the news lead us to despair, because we complete the news with God's half. Christians are the truest messengers of hope, because we can see most clearly what the world and life and human beings are all about.

Twenty-Twenty Vision of God

Most of us do not have perfect vision in both eyes. One eye is usually weaker than the other and may need a corrective lens. In the same way, our spiritual vision unquestionably needs a stronger corrective lens than our natural vision.

What most often needs correction in my spiritual perspective is my view of God. The strength of my hidden life—including my ability to rest internally, trust radically and live for Christ unreservedly—depends more on how I view Him than on anything else.

Here I have to be ruthlessly honest. In my selfish moments, which are many, I want God to look and act in a certain way. I want Him to make life work well for me and for the ones I love.

But even in my unselfish moments, when I actually care more for His reputation than my happiness, I still have an idea of how He should appear in the world. I want Him to show everyone that He is a God of justice, that He answers prayer, that He is worthy of trust. Would this not give Him the greatest glory?

When I think this way, the words God spoke to Moses in their first conversation echo in my ears: "I am who I am" (Exod. 3:14). Not, as a friend once reminded me, "I am who you want Me to be."

Through years of walking with God, letting Him correct my vision, I have learned two hardly won lessons: I cannot control God by my prayers; and I am not to define Him by my circumstances.

God's view of my life is clearer and broader than mine. As such, He may well say no to my requests, no matter how fervent my prayers. We give our hearts to God through prayer, and we believe Him for great things because He is a great God; but in the end, "the language of heaven is 'Thy will be done.'"

When what happens to me does not agree with my understanding of God, will it distort my vision of Him? Will I stop praying because He let the thing happen which I prayed so fervently against? Will I stop trusting because He has not yet answered the prayer I have prayed for a long, long time? Or will I see God through a clearer, purer medium than the distorted one of my own situation?

Dan DeHaan gives a helpful illustration of correctly seeing God in his book *The God You Can Know*:

If we were to take a stick and put it into a glass of water, it would seem to be crooked. Why? Because we look at it through two mediums—air and water. It is the same with our understanding of God. His various characteristics, such as His justice, seem crooked to us. The wicked seem to prosper and the righteous suffer. It seems that unfair events take place all the time. The problem is not with God but with us. We view God's proceedings through a double medium of flesh and spirit. Therefore, it is not that God's character is bent, it is that man is not competent to judge.[1]

Put a stick in water and its image is distorted. If I want to see the stick's true form, I need to pull it out of the water and see it through the one medium that shows its truest form, which happens to be air. In the same way, I cannot rely on circumstances to give a clear representation of God.

If I allow the happenings of my life to shape my view of God, then I will change my opinion of Him constantly. *When life is good, God is kind; when life is painful, He doesn't care. My friend is healed of cancer, so prayer works; my friend dies, so God doesn't hear. My nephew returns home safely from Iraq, therefore God is trustworthy; my nephew is killed though I prayed daily for his safety, therefore God cannot be trusted.*

To see properly, we must see God through the one true medium of His Word.

We do not see God clearly this way. To see properly, we must see Him through the one true medium of His Word. When we judge God by what happens to us, we are telling Him who He is. But in His Word, He speaks for Himself.

As our vision of God is corrected, the events in our lives become clearer. A friend once said, "Our disappointments are God's appointments." Our difficulties are actually God's opportunities.

Disappointment and difficulty show only half the picture. Appointment and opportunity reveal God's half. This gives hope and certainty to a world that desperately needs to know that Someone loving and wise knows what He is doing.

A Personal Journey

If we want to know which world we view most clearly, our reactions will show us. What do we do when "life happens while we're making other plans"?

If you are like me, after the initial reaction of surprise or frustration or disbelief, you manage to calm down and think about the problem that has just come your way. You analyze it, discuss it with others and at some point in the process remember to look to God.

Thankfully, He is strengthening my spiritual vision, and more and more quickly I am able to bring temporal and eternal realities together.

I remember one late June afternoon the summer before Scott's freshman year at college. Our family had just returned from Chad to get him ready for this next big step in his life.

Scott had been accepted at the University of North Carolina through early admission, but he had done all his college preparation from Germany where he was attending high school. This included online registration for campus housing.

The deadline for housing notification was in June, so we were not too concerned when he had not yet received his assignment by graduation in May. But we began to worry as May drew to a close and there was still no word. Once back in America, we called the housing office to ask about the delay.

"Your son's name?" asked the voice on the other end of the line.

We gave Scott's full name to make sure they found his information. There was a noticeable pause and then, "Well, I'm sorry, but he's not on the list."

We were stunned. Scott had registered for housing early in January, giving him several months' head start on other applicants. And now we were told he was not even in the system.

We assured the woman on the phone that he had done his part and, in our minds, deserved their help, but she merely repeated again that his name was not in the system. She was sorry, but since he had no place on campus, he would have to find housing elsewhere.

Our first response was shock. The second was anger. Thankfully we had hung up by this time and not expressed it to the poor woman who was simply doing her job as a secretary. But we were quick to blame someone or something. Cyberspace was a mess, having obviously swallowed up the online registration. God was not watching out for Scott, having obviously let this one slip. The university was a faceless unsympathetic voice thwarting our well-laid plans for our son's freshman year.

Louis and I had both attended the university. This was where we had met, and we loved it—until now. Suddenly it was large, impersonal, incompetent and extremely uncaring about its students. We vented our frustration, ending with a panicked cry not unlike Elisha's servant: "What shall we do?"

After about five minutes of that, however, we remembered something—or rather, Someone. God was aware of the situation and had been all along. If anyone could fix it, He could.

Before any further discussion, we called Scott to join us,

bowed our heads together and prayed. Louis and I asked God's forgiveness for leaving Him out of the situation and reacting as if He had let something slip through His fingers. We would trust Him to work on Scott's behalf, even if the situation did not look good from our perspective.

When we lifted our heads, the physical circumstances had not changed. But we had brought God in to complete the picture. We got up from our knees with hearts prepared to trust.

Looking to God for help was nothing new for us. We had faced rebel fire, a black mamba under the bed, a daughter's serious illness and the challenge of crossing flowing rivers in the rainy season. The difficulties of living in Chad put an online housing blip in perspective.

We had also seen God's faithfulness over and over again, but we were much too quick to forget past faithfulness

Had we not prayed for months? Was not God a good Father who wants good things for His children?

when staring at a present problem. We were thankful that in the aftershock of the news, it took only five minutes before we bowed our heads and talked to God; but it was a reminder that we still had impaired vision.

I had more to learn in the days ahead about seeing God with twenty-twenty vision. With only two months available to find on-campus housing for Scott, we continued to pray and asked others to pray. And we did our part, knowing that God does not usually steer a parked car. Scott put his name on the waiting list, and we made phone calls to people who might influence the housing office. Eventually, knowing our time was short, we began looking for an apartment.

I wanted more than anything else for Scott to find a place on campus. I had great memories from my years at this same university and wanted my son to have the same positive beginning to campus life.

Had we not prayed since his acceptance in December for a good transition to college in America after living the majority of his life overseas? Had we not prayed for months for his roommate? Was not God a good Father who wants good things for His children, and was He not all-powerful?

When there was still no word from campus housing by early August, Scott accepted an offer to share an apartment with two other students, another freshman and a senior. We signed the lease on Saturday morning.

On Monday morning we received a call from the university. They had a place for Scott in one of the dorms if he still needed it.

I was more than stunned this time. I was confused. Clearly, God was off in His timing. He had answered our prayers for campus housing, but was late by forty-eight hours. We were on our way to the bank to set up an account for Scott when the university called, so we told the voice on the phone no, but thank you, hung up politely and headed out the door.

As we drove, I imagined the faceless voice drawing a line through my son's name and picking up the phone to call the next student on the list—the student who would get that place on campus.

When we reached the bank, I asked Louis and Scott to

go in without me. My mind was still reacting to the news, and I needed to sit in the car and talk it through with God. Writing keeps me focused, so I pulled a notepad and pen out of my purse and wrote what was on my heart. The real me came to the real God, sitting in my car in a parking lot.

"You *knew* this was coming, Lord. Why did You let us sign the lease on Saturday? Why did you not stop us in some way?"

I find that the more one believes in God's sovereignty, the harder it is to accept the things that look wrong this side of heaven. The problem is not with God's sovereignty, however, but with my idea of what His sovereignty should look like.

What I think looks wrong may be very right from His point of view. My perspective of His goodness may not fit His description of good. The Lord's voice, quiet as a whisper and soft as a gentle nudge, broke into my writing.

"You're right, I did know this would happen."

I sat back, let the pen fall slack in my hand and closed my eyes.

"Yes, Lord, of course. Thank You for reminding me."

God's timing was not off. It was right on target for His arrangement of Scott's first year of college. Sitting in the car talking things through with God, I realized that once again my vision was impaired. I was looking at one half of the picture and seeing bad timing. God reminded me to look at His half and see His plan at work.

Something else needed to change in my view of the situation, and that was my idea of what was best for Scott's freshman year. God had answered prayer for housing, but not according to my fixed ideas. Now I had to face the fact that I did not like His answer.

Here was an opportunity for a deeper work God wanted to do in me. I needed to die to my own ideas. I needed to let go of my plan, my preferred choice, and trust God for His.

"Lord, You know better than I what Scott needs for this coming year. More than anything else, more than the housing, what I really want is for him to grow close to You. I trust You to know what he needs for that to happen."

Two things happened during this conversation. A disappointment became His appointment, and a desire to control became an opportunity to trust. Neither can happen unless I see both God and my situation through eyes of faith.

Hindsight is twenty-twenty vision, as we often hear, and that was certainly true in this case. Because of living in an apartment, Scott joined a Christian fellowship for off-campus students. Through this group he met four guys who shared another apartment, one in which the fellowship often gathered.

"The view is much better from up here," God says. "Trust Me to do what is best."

When one of the four guys graduated at the end of the year, Scott was invited to take his place. For his remaining college years he shared that apartment with these three young men, who became his closest friends. They held each other accountable as Christians and all became leaders in some capacity in the fellowship.

God was answering my deeper prayer for Scott's growth in Christ. He and his roommates became such close friends that Louis and I called them "the band of brothers." Even more significant, Scott met someone else who attended the off-campus fellowship—the lovely young woman who is now our daughter-in-law.

God has what I call "the eagle's point of view." As the eagle sees an entire landscape from the heights where it flies, God sees the entire map of our lives—past, present, future. That morning in the car, I saw only a dot on the map marked "You are here: bad timing/withheld desire."

I see now that God certainly knew what He was doing. He knew *where* He wanted Scott to be in order to bring *who* He wanted into his life. That morning in the parking lot, however, I had to rise up to eagles' heights and trust another pair of eyes. "The view is much better from up here," God says. "Trust Me to do what is best."

Hidden Treasures

We miss something wonderful when we see only our half of the picture. Anne Graham Lotz tells the story of receiving a present from her mother in the mail. Inside the box was a rather gaudy basket filled with crumpled paper, which surprised her since it was not the kind of thing her mother would normally give.

Anne tossed the paper into the trash before phoning to thank her mother, only to be told that the real gift was in the paper! Thankfully, she was able to retrieve the pieces quickly and uncover the beautiful ring hidden carefully inside. She nearly missed the true gift by seeing no further than what immediately met her eyes.

A.B. Simpson, founder of the Christian and Missionary Alliance, encouraged us to see two realities in everything that comes our way:

There are secrets of providence which God's dear children may learn. His dealings with them often seem, to the outward eye, dark and terrible. Faith looks deeper and says, "This is God's secret. You look only on the outside; I can look deeper and see the hidden meaning."

Sometimes diamonds are done up in rough packages, so that their value cannot be seen. When the tabernacle was built in the wilderness there was nothing rich in its outside appearance. The costly things were all within, and its outward covering of rough badger skin gave no hint of the valuable things which it contained.

God may send you, dear friends, some costly packages. Do not worry if they are done up in rough wrappings. You may be sure there are treasures of love, and kindness, and wisdom hidden within. If we take what he sends, and trust him for the goodness in it, even in the dark, we shall learn the meaning of the secrets of providence.[2]

Heart Beats

The heart that listens:

How does seeing with the eyes of faith, according to these verses, affect my decision making, my level of confidence, my priorities, the state of my heart and my responses?

Psalm 27:13–14   Mark 13:31
Psalm 73:16–17   John 16:33
Isaiah 26:3–4   Romans 8:28
Isaiah 48:17–18   Hebrews 11:1–3
Matthew 6:25–34

The heart that responds:

Read the following poem by George MacDonald as a prayer:

Lord, loosen in me the hold of visible things;
Help me to walk by faith and not by sight;
I would, through thickest veils and coverings,
See into the chambers of the living light.
Lord, in the land of things that swell and seem,
Help me to walk by the other light supreme,
Which shows Thy facts behind man's vaguely hinting dream.[3]

Believing

Lord, do with us, not only outwardly, but deep within us,
as it seems good to you. (*François Fénelon*)

Be transformed by the renewing of your mind. (*Romans 12:2*)

*O*live groves and fig trees
abound in the Middle East, so it is no wonder Jesus used
such illustrations to explain spiritual realities. In an agricultural society, listeners needed only a glance around to grasp
what Jesus meant when He said, "No good tree bears bad
fruit, nor does a bad tree bear good fruit. Each tree is recognized by its own fruit. People do not pick figs from thornbushes, or grapes from briers" (Luke 6:43–44). These words
came alive to us during our years in Chad.

A variety of trees grew in our yard. We are not experts in
agriculture, but we were able to definitively classify the tree
with lemons hanging from its branches as a lemon tree. We
had no clue as to the identity of another tree in the yard,

because it bore no fruit, at least not immediately. We imagined it might produce guavas or even, on a hopeful long shot, oranges.

We asked a Chadian friend to identify the unknown tree. His answer did not help, since in our early days of language study, with our limited Arabic, we translated everything literally. *Fuwakih hanna mahabba*—fruit of love? Only after it finally produced did we realize it was a passion fruit tree.

> A tree's identity is revealed by its fruit. The world will measure whether or not we are Christians by the way we live.

A tree's identity is revealed by its fruit, and we were finally able to name the one in our yard by what we observed on its branches. Jesus further clarified this principle of identification in a later discussion with His disciples:

> As I have loved you, so you must love one another. By this all men will know that you are my disciples, if you love one another. (John 13:34–35)

> This is to my Father's glory, that you bear much fruit, showing yourselves to be my disciples. (John 15:8)

Jesus says that the world will measure whether or not we are true Christians by the way we live—and especially by our degree of Christlike love. "Not many people will read the Bible," I have heard it said, "but they will read our lives."

Many people listening to Jesus exhibited forms of religious life which identified them as "good" Jews. They went to the synagogue, listened to teaching from the Torah, tithed and observed religious feasts. But they were far from spiritual health.

Jesus, as always, was interested in the heart. He continued his illustration: "The good man brings good things out of the good stored up in his heart, and the evil man brings evil things out of the evil stored up in his heart. For out of the overflow of his heart his mouth speaks" (Luke 6:45).

Fruit, whether on trees or in people, is the expression of true character. And our character stems from what we truly believe. Religious behavior, if it does not spring from right believing, is nothing more than a false presentation.

False Fruit

Jesus told a parable about a man who planted a fig tree in his vineyard. After three years of producing nothing, the tree was ordered cut down by the owner of the vineyard. It was not bearing fruit, so it was not worth keeping.

The caretaker of the vineyard, however, was not ready to give up on the tree. He persuaded the owner to give it another chance. "Leave it alone for one more year, and I'll dig around it and fertilize it. If it bears fruit next year, fine! If not, then cut it down" (Luke 13:8–9).

The parable ends at this point, and we have no idea what happened to the tree at the end of that year. However, we can imagine some possible sequels.

Having lived in a culture where life does not work by schedules and people with good intentions do not always follow through, I can envision an interesting scenario.

The year has rolled around and it is time for the owner's return. Where has the time gone?! Despite the gardener's good intentions, he has not worked on the tree, and it is still not producing. What can he do to convince the owner it is worth keeping?

An idea comes to mind, born of desperation, because he wants to keep the tree as well as the owner's good opinion of him. The gardener runs to the market, buys a basket of figs and a tube of super glue, and rushes back to carefully glue figs to the tree's branches. He steps back to observe his handiwork.

This may just do the trick. If the master arrives when expected—and if the gardener can keep him from looking too closely—at first glance he will think the tree has finally begun to produce. The servant nods his head in satisfaction and waits for the owner to arrive.

Since in non-Western cultures life does not move by the clock, a month or even two can go by beyond an expected arrival date. But, at long last, the owner shows up to check on his vineyard. What does he find? Not evidence of a healthy tree producing healthy fruit, certainly. Instead, he observes withering fruit attached to the branches.

In this speculative ending, the caretaker's efforts hid the true nature of the situation. Even if the owner had arrived as scheduled and seen fresh figs on the tree, the fruit would not have lasted because it had no connection to the life source. It was not the real thing.

The Root of the Matter

Another possible conclusion to the parable does not require such a creative conceptualization. We can imagine that the caretaker did his job and focused on improving the life of the tree. He dug around the roots. He loosened the hardened ground, pulling out weeds and rocks that hindered growth. Then he added fertilizer to the soil to stimulate growth. Both *pulling out* and *putting in* were necessary.

The problem is that when we apply these principles to ourselves, we often think once more in terms of our behavior. We determine to stop bad habits and start healthy ones. Again, this does not reach the source of the problem—which is rooted in what we are truly convinced of.

> *Lasting change happens from the inside out. Do not merely change what you do. Change what you believe.*

Lasting change can only come from deep within. Only when we change our thinking—our belief system—will we change how we act.

The apostle Paul understood this. We are transformed through the *renewal of our minds*, he wrote to the church in Rome (see Rom. 12:2). To the Ephesians he wrote, "Put off your old self, which is being corrupted by its deceitful desires; . . . *be made new in the attitude of your minds*; and . . . put on the new self, created to be like God in true righteousness and holiness" (Eph. 4:22–24). And in a letter to the Colossians, Paul equated putting on the new self with a renewed mind (see Col. 3:10).

The twin acts of putting off the old and putting on the new might imply something we do outwardly, such as the changing of clothes. But Paul is writing about a change of mind. Lasting change happens from the inside out. Do not merely change what you do, Paul writes. Change what you believe.

Dallas Willard, professor of philosophy at the University of Southern California and author of excellent books on inner transformation, writes about this change. He observes:

> One of the greatest weaknesses in our teaching and leadership today is that we spend so much time trying to get people to do things good people are supposed to do, without changing what they really believe. It doesn't succeed very well, and that is the open secret of church life. We frankly need to do much less of this managing of action, and especially with young people. We need to concentrate on changing the minds of those we would reach and serve. What they do will certainly follow, as Jesus well understood and taught.[1]

Though Willard does advocate spiritual disciplines to develop our faith (and I must say emphatically that I do too), I agree with his observations on our need for heart change:

> The emphasis is all too often on some point of behavior modification. This is helpful, but it is not adequate to human life. It does not reach the root of the human problem. *That root is the character of the inner life*, where Jesus and his call to apprenticeship in the kingdom place the emphasis.[2]

E.M. Bounds, a turn-of-the-century lawyer-turned-pastor and devotional writer, would have concurred. In his classic work on prayer, he wrote, "Conduct is what we do, character is what we are. Conduct is the outward life. Character is the unseen life that is hidden within, yet shown by what we do."[3]

How then do we accomplish this change?

I Believe!

First, we must *discover* what we believe. The discovery process may produce some surprises, because our true beliefs are not always what we think they are.

This is especially important for church members who have been told what they should think. Such Christians have an answer when asked about doctrine, yet their actions may not always correspond with their words. This is significant. No matter what we say, our responses to life reveal what we are convinced of deep within.

Louis discovered this one summer in Kansas City.

During his college years, Louis spent a summer internship working with the Kansas City police force. The program included a shift with each department, which was why he found himself one day flying high above the city in a helicopter. Fascinated by the new experience, Louis asked the pilot a multitude of questions, including what would happen if the engine cut off while they were in the air.

That would be no problem, the pilot explained, because of autorotation. If the engine failed, the propellers would continue to rotate because of upward wind flow, and the helicopter could make a controlled descent.

Louis said, "Mmmhmm."

The pilot glanced at him and said, "You don't believe me, do you?"

Louis assured him he did.

"No," the pilot said. "You don't believe me."

"Yes, I do! I believe you."

"No, you don't," the pilot said. He reached over, turned off the engine and leaned calmly back with his arms crossed.

The descending helicopter was too much for Louis, even with the relaxed smile on the pilot's face. He grabbed his seat and yelled, "I believe! I believe! Turn it back on!"

Louis laughs about it now, but the question remains: Which of the men trusted in autorotation? Louis said he did, but his reaction showed otherwise. The pilot was certain enough to turn off the engine.

Our true belief system is lodged in the core of our being. This is the root of our behavior, affecting our relationships and responses to life.

> We may or may not be aware of them. Many core beliefs are lived out but not thought out. Our core beliefs are demonstrated not by what we say they are, but how we live them out. . . . When a core belief accurately reflects truth and reality, it motivates us to act appropriately and effectively. Of course the opposite is true also; some of our core beliefs may be false, and so lead us to act inappropriately.[4]

When our deepest convictions are based on error, they produce unhealthy behavior. False understanding keeps us right where the Enemy wants us: trapped by his lies rather than living in the freedom and fullness of God's truth.

Our reactions to life are like bubbles on the surface of a lake that indicate something underneath.[5] Or, to keep the metaphor of the tree, they are like a thorn that suddenly sprouts on what we thought was a fig tree.

Our reactions often take us by surprise. *Where did that come from?* we wonder. *Why did I feel so offended at her criti-*

cism? I don't know why I get so angry when my child misbehaves in church—he's only three years old! Why do I feel annoyed when she talks so much?

Anger, defensiveness, critical and judgmental feelings—even irritation at someone else's personality— are fruits of what we hold to be true. They influence us far more than we realize. That's why identifying them is vital.

If we are open to the Spirit's work, we can trace our reactions to their source.

"Pulling Out" What Hinders Growth

If we are open to the Spirit's work, we can trace our reactions to their source. The caretaker in the parable (assuming he followed through on his intentions) tended to the tree's health by digging around it and then fertilizing. We can dig for unhealthy roots by asking a series of questions beginning with "why"—until we reach the belief that motivated the action, reaction, thought or feeling.

All the lies we accept are as old as the Garden. "God cannot be trusted," whispers the Enemy. "You are deficient as you are. You need more in life that what God has ordained for you. You are the star of the show."

I was extremely anxious about speaking in front of a group, and I wondered why, since I had spoken many times before. The night before the meeting, I could not sleep for thinking of the message I was to give in the morning. So I lay on the bed and talked it over with God.

Uncovering the deception that produces anxiety can be as simple as "entering the tent" for personal conversation with God. This is practical, and, with the Spirit keeping us honest, it is effective. Getting up close and personal is the key. We must be willing to be genuine with ourselves and with God, real enough to push through shallow answers until we get to root causes. For me, asking and answering the "why" questions in God's presence went something like this:

Why am I so nervous about speaking?

Because I could do a poor job.

Why does it matter if I do a poor job?

Because I want to honor You, Lord, and a poorly done message won't honor You.

The truth is that God's honor is not tied to my ability to speak. I knew this but still felt anxious. God too was perfectly aware that as sincere as I am about honoring Him, fear of failure for His sake was not really the source of my anxiety. I needed to ask more questions.

So again, what if I do a poor job?

Why would that matter?

Because it will be embarrassing.

People will think poorly of me.

Why does it matter what others think of me?

Because what others think of me matters to me.

And why is that? Because how others think of me says something about who I am.

I finally arrived at a core belief that determined how I was responding. *I am what others think of me.* Through a series of questions in which I was willing to be honest, I uncovered a lie. Eve believed the same one. She did not rest in what God thought of her, but listened to Satan's deceit.

I am what others think of me. No wonder I was nervous about speaking in front of a group whose impression of me would come from how I deliver a thirty minute message. No wonder I feared failure as a speaker. If my value as a person rested on my speaking performance, then I had to perform well or be judged deficient.

Absurd, yes—and if you had asked me where my worth lay before I discussed it with God, I would have given the answer I "knew" was true, but it wouldn't have reflected what I actually believed. I would have told you that my identity and worth are found in Christ, not in the opinions of others. Doesn't the Bible say, "Man looks at the outward appearance, but the LORD looks at the heart" (1 Sam. 16:7)?

Yet the thorny "fruit" revealed evidence of something false within. The fruit of believing a deception brought self-centered stress rather than Christ-centered rest.

Another lie at work was that *I* was the focus of the speaking engagement, and I had to dig that one out as well. As a speaker, I wanted to have something worth saying—partly from a sincere desire to speak truth, yes, but also because there were seasoned leaders from our mission in the group. They will laugh to think I ever considered them in such a way, but they were spiritual giants in my mind at the time. What could I possibly say to them?

Lord, I prayed, *I have nothing to give them that they don't already know.*

"You are not giving it to them. I am. Just bring them to Me," was the answer.

Yes, I thought. *I can do that. I can bring them to You; that's all I need to do.*

Returning the focus to Christ calmed my heart. I actually slept well that night, and the next morning I looked forward to bringing the group to Christ through the passage He had given me to share. I was not a speaker with a message but a waiter serving what God had prepared for His people. Spotlight on Christ and not on self.

"While we are looking at God, we do not see ourselves. Blessed riddance," wrote A.W. Tozer. The result of focus on Christ is freedom from self and a soul that rests from concern about the opinions of others.

Dealing with Exposed Roots

Tracing our reactions to their source enables us to deal with them. But once uncovered, what do we do with them?

First, we can do *nothing* apart from Christ. We must take our unbelief to the One who alone can change us.

> *We can do nothing apart from Christ. We must take our unbelief to the One who alone can change us.*

Then we come to God in confession and repentance. We admit that despite what we have said with our lips, we have not truly believed His Word. Like Eve, we have listened to the Enemy of our souls and have allowed a lie to control how we live.

Third, we ask forgiveness.

And finally, we take God at His Word when He says, "If we confess our sins, he is faithful and just and will forgive us our sins and purify us from all unrighteousness" (1 John 1:9).

But what if you are not sure you can change what you

believe? Or you are afraid of what change will require?

A man brought his son to Jesus for healing and said, "If you can do anything, take pity on us and help us."

"'"If you can"?' said Jesus. 'Everything is possible for him who believes.'"

The father's answer should encourage all of us who struggle with our faith. He immediately exclaimed, "I do believe; help me overcome my unbelief!" (Mark 9:22–24).

What is significant in this encounter is that Jesus accepted the father as he was. He accepts us too. Jesus does not ask us to change before we come to Him. He asks us to come as we are, and He will change us.

"Putting In" to Stimulate Growth

Digging out false convictions through confession and repentance is the beginning of change. But this process must continue by developing a faith in what is true. The caretaker not only dug around the tree, but he fertilized it to encourage growth. We fertilize the soul by "putting in" more and more of God's Word.

Who does God say I am as a Christian? How does He see me?

We open His Word. We ask Him to show us. He "puts in" the truth and speaks to us through a study of His Father-heart or His Lordship. We learn that we are children, witnesses, disciples, servants, saints. We learn that we are "crucified with Christ"; that we "no longer live" but that Christ lives in us; and that Christ within is changing us by His Spirit. We learn that there is hope for people in process.

The helicopter pilot was not born believing in autorotation. There was a time when he too needed to step out in faith and trust the flight manual. Then experience made words on a page come to life.

When we, like Moses, come into God's presence, we go beyond studying words on a page to experiencing real life with God. Over time we trust the words not because we are supposed to, but because we know the One who spoke them. We know His Word is true because we know God is true.

What We Believe about God

Of all the things we believe in the core of our being, it's what we believe about God Himself that affects our behavior more than anything else. Our reactions to what God allows in our lives will betray what we truly think of Him.

Martha Kilpatrick writes in her book *Adoration*, "We are always exposed by how we accuse God." Is He good only when things are going well? Is He loving and wise only when life makes sense, when my prayers are answered, when justice is done?

In the past thirty years of my relationship with God, I have experienced carefully laid plans uprooted by His timing, fervent prayers that seemed to go unanswered and circumstances jarring my understanding of His character.

In her poem "Martha vs. Mary," Kilpatrick presents these challenging words:

> Jesus is always commandeered
> to obey those
> who *work* for Him,
> but those who sit in abasement
> at His feet . . .
> let Him be *Himself.*[6]

Martha was busy working for Jesus, frustrated that Mary merely sat at His feet. She accused Jesus of not caring for her and commanded Him to make Mary get up and help (see Luke 10:38–42). What would have happened if Martha had traced her frustration and irritation to the core belief that influenced her attitudes?

Maybe we can ask her when we meet in heaven. But it does seem, as the poem suggests, that she had her own idea of how Jesus should care for her.

We too may have similar expectations. We profess that He is good, but deep down our convictions define how that goodness should look. It does not include being fired from a job or being paralyzed by an accident. Like Martha, we have our own ways of demanding, "If You really cared for me, God, You would . . ."

The more we know God, the more we will trust Him— despite what we see.

While Martha was diligently working for Jesus, Mary was getting to know Him. The more we know God, the more we will trust Him—despite what we see.

Trusting What We Know

My deepest beliefs about God were challenged again when "life happened" to someone I care deeply about. Unlike my conversation with God about my nervousness to speak, this situation did not end in the way I like to define goodness.

My sister Meg is truly one of the best people I know. But she endured months of slander and nearly three years of prison for something she did not do.

Meg was a lawyer and judge who ran for political office and won as Commissioner of Agriculture in the state of North Carolina. During her campaign, she intentionally kept a distance from financial details. Not wanting to be influenced by donations if she were elected to office, she left monetary issues to her campaign treasurer.

That decision, motivated by integrity, led to her undoing.

Meg served for one year in office before charges of corruption were brought against her campaign. As the trial unfolded, there was evidence of corruption from members of her campaign staff.

Even so, contradicting stories from witnesses and evidence that one of Meg's staff members had stolen campaign funds for personal use did not faze the prosecutors. There was a political agenda at work overriding the pursuit of truth. Meg was the big fish the prosecutors wanted, not her staff. Since it was her campaign, she was guilty.

I attended every day of the court proceedings and prayed more passionately than I had prayed for anything since an illness of our daughter's years earlier. Taking God at His Word, I prayed the Scriptures and trusted that a God of justice would not let my sister be a victim of injustice.

During the trial there was evidence of His faithfulness in small ways. But the prayer that God said no to was the main one of my heart—that Meg would be declared innocent. A political agenda won the day.

The final verdict hit like a train, and it took some time to stand up again after the blow. I can still remember the moment Meg was declared guilty. She turned to her husband Robert, whispered, "I love you," and was taken, handcuffed, from the courtroom.

The next day I was physically and emotionally exhausted. I was too numb to pray and could only sit with my legs pulled up in an armchair, listening to worship music. My thoughts followed a deep conviction of my heart: "I know Meg is innocent, because I know her. I know her character. I know her heart. It doesn't matter what anyone else says—most of all the media—because I know her."

I wrestled with the fact that a just God had allowed such abuse despite fervent and faith-filled prayers. Then He broke into my thoughts with quiet yet powerful words. *You believe Meg because you know her. You owe Me the same, because you know Me.*

Well, Lord, I shot back, *it's a good thing I've known You for thirty years, because from what I see You don't look very good right now.*

True friends in dialogue can handle candor, and God can handle ours. He wants us to be real with Him. We certainly cannot tell Him something He does not already know, since He sees the heart. It's we who need to face our need with honesty before Him.

Open dialogue opens the door for genuine growth. God can deal with our doubts as well as our fears and confusion. The important thing is what we do with them. We need to take the questions of our heart to Him and wait for His answers.

A week later, some close friends invited Louis and me to their beach house so we could rest and process what had happened. One afternoon on the beach, I had a long and very loud conversation with God. It included tears, questions and accusations, but also a listening ear to His voice.

Going to God with my anger and confusion was what I needed to begin regaining my footing.

God was right in saying I owed Him the same trust I so readily gave my sister. I was fully persuaded of Meg's integrity because I knew her personally. I did this so easily for someone I could see—and yet God was just as real as Meg. After thirty years of life with God, I could trust Him because I knew Him.

Okay, Lord, I prayed in the end, *I will trust You even in this. You have the bigger picture. You know what You want to do in Meg's life and where You want her to be. I wish it did not include this, but I will trust You in it.*

My sister also knows God, and she chose to trust Him as well. During her years in prison, we both looked to God's Word and drew encouragement from what we found. Joseph was a victim of injustice yet lived to understand the "why" (see Gen. 50:15–21). Job suffered unimaginable and irreplaceable losses yet could fall to the ground and worship (see Job 1). Habakkuk saw what was happening in the world and still chose to praise and trust a sovereign God (see Hab. 3:17–19).

Believing God when we do not yet see the good He intends is to trust Him in the dark. That deeper faith honors Him above all.

What do *you* truly believe about God, about yourself, about the world we live in? How would taking God at His Word, despite what you see, affect your life? Are you willing to act on what you know to be true—even if those around you do not understand your response of faith?

The lasting fruit of taking God at His Word is a soul at rest—looking much like the helicopter pilot who sat back and smiled when the engine cut off. Autorotation was real, and he knew it. Believing and trusting made all the difference.

Heart Beats

What things is your mind set on most? You must answer that question. It will determine your entire character. (*Dan DeHaan*)[7]

The heart that listens:

Read the following verses and let God speak to you about taking Him at His Word.

Isaiah 43:10
Mark 5:35–36
Mark 9:21–24
John 4:39–42
John 20:24–29

How would believing God affect the way you are living your life?

The heart that responds:

Be alert to "bubbles" on the surface of your life in the coming weeks:

• The next time you react to something in an unhealthy

way or in a way that surprises you, take time in God's presence to trace the surface reaction to its source.

- Ask God to reveal the false belief or self-life that motivated this reaction.

- Once uncovered, admit it to God and ask His forgiveness. If there is evidence of self-life (pride, self-promotion, self-pity, etc.), ask for His transformation from self-focus to Christ focus.

- Do a personal study of God's characteristics that counter the lie you have accepted. If possible, ask a friend to study with you, keeping you accountable to change the source of your responses to life.

-9-

Soaring

All creatures that have wings can escape from every snare that is set for them if they will only fly high enough. (*Hannah Whitall Smith*)

They will soar on wings like eagles. (*Isaiah 40:31*)

*B*irds fly overhead, and I follow their movements with my eyes. I am once again in the backyard enjoying time out from public life at the front door. The birds move in circles, dipping and diving as though playing on an invisible airfield, and I envy their ability to defy the law of gravity. I want to soar with them, but I have no wings.

Restlessness and dissatisfaction have kept people trying to take flight for centuries, from Leonardo da Vinci's fifteenth-century flying machines to the first hot air balloon launched in the 1700s (the passengers were a sheep, a duck and a rooster) to the Wright brothers at Kitty Hawk in 1903.

We can now glide above the clouds in a flying machine, but *we* have still not learned how to fly. God has left that to the birds.

Or has He?

The truth is, while physically we are bound by the law of gravity, spiritually we were created to soar. Our longing to fly is really a desire for God. But circumstances can work on our spirit like gravity works on our bodies. Have you noticed? No matter how high we jump, they keep pulling us down. Our reactions to them, whether doubt, fear, anxiety, discouragement, bitterness or despair, keep us earthbound—tied down when God means for us to rise above.

> You will keep in perfect peace
>   him whose mind is steadfast,
>   because he trusts in you. (Isa. 26:3)

> This is what the sovereign LORD, the Holy One of Israel, says:
>   "In repentance and rest is your salvation,
>   in quietness and trust is your strength." (Isa. 30:15)

> The fruit of righteousness will be peace;
>   the effect of righteousness will be
>   quietness and confidence forever.
> My people will live in peaceful dwelling places,
>   in secure homes,
>   in undisturbed places of rest. (Isa. 32:17–18)

Perfect peace. Quietness and confidence. Undisturbed rest. How do we get there? How do we rise above the demands of life, the heartbreaks of lost relationships, the pressures of difficult decisions—and overcome?

God has provided a way for the heart and mind to defy

the downward pull of circumstances. He has given us wings to fly if we will only use them.

> Those who hope in the LORD
>> will renew their strength.
>> They will soar on wings like eagles;
>> they will run and not grow weary,
>> they will walk and not be faint. (Isa. 40:31)

I love God's choice of the eagle as an image of renewed strength. All birds fly, but not all fly as high as the eagle. Smaller birds dart from tree to tree in fits and starts, flapping and fluttering their wings in what seems a laborious effort to get from point A to point B.

Eagles, however, glide on invisible currents of air, soaring above mountains where the view is spectacular. God gives us eagles' wings, as well; and with them we can soar to greater heights, renew our strength and gain a clearer perspective.

Eagle's Point of View

Imagine a man walking a trail in the valley and an eagle flying high above him. The man sees his immediate surroundings. He can see the path in front of him, but he cannot see around the bend on the trail.

If he had a map, the man would see only the red dot marking his location. But the eagle, soaring on the heights, sees the entire landscape. It sees beyond the bend in the road as well as the stream, a mile away, that the man wants to reach. The eagle has a view of the full picture and (if it could think in such terms) knows exactly how the man should proceed.

Like that man, I cannot see what is ahead. I do not know what God has in mind for the rest of my journey. I see only my "red dot." It says, "You are here"—in the middle of a bad situation, discouraged by unanswered prayer, dealing with a disappointment.

God, however, has a much better view of my path. He sees the entire course of my life. He knows where I need to be at the end of my journey, spiritually, emotionally and physically. And most importantly, He knows how I need to get there. My position may not look good from my limited point of view, but from God's perspective, it is necessary.

Joseph could have become a bitter man. Instead, he became a thankful man.

F.B. Meyer writes, "Do not look from earth towards heaven but from heaven towards earth. Let God, not man, be your standpoint of vision."[1] Joseph had this heaven-to-earth vision, and it helped him rise above the things in his life that did not look good at all.

Joseph's early years contained a string of distressing events and setbacks brought about by others. His brothers envied him and sold him into slavery; his boss's wife slandered him and her false accusation landed him in prison; a released prison mate promised to plead his case but forgot him instead. Hated, misrepresented, imprisoned and disappointed by broken promises, Joseph could easily have become a bitter man. Instead, he became a thankful man.

What happened? He understood that God was in control of his circumstances, even the difficult and disappointing ones. Instead of being crushed by them, he saw God's hand at work in each one, using his experiences as stepping stones to bring him to service in greater ways than he could have planned or imagined on his own.

When he was reunited with his brothers after many years, they were terrified he would want revenge for what they had done to him so many years before. But Joseph was not tied down to the hurts of his past. He had risen above them and gained the eagle's point of view. "You intended to harm me, but God intended it for good to accomplish what is now being done, the saving of many lives" (Gen. 50:20).

Hannah Hurnard, in the introduction to her wonderful allegory of journeying with Christ, *Hinds Feet on High Places*, presents this perspective:

> As Christians we know, in theory at least, that in the life of a child of God there are no second causes, that even the most unjust and cruel things, as well as all seemingly point-less and undeserved sufferings have been permitted by God as a glorious opportunity for us to react to them in such a way that our Lord and Savior is able to produce in us, little by little, his own lovely character.[2]

Eagle's Wings

God has given us wings to soar above our circumstances and gain the eagle's point of view. What are they, then, and how do we use them? Hannah Whitall Smith, in her classic volume *The Christian's Secret of a Happy Life,* writes about living above the things happening around us:

> The soul that waits upon the Lord is the soul that is en-tirely surrendered to Him, and that trusts Him perfectly.

Therefore we might name our wings the wings of Surrender and of Trust. I mean by this, that if we will only surrender ourselves utterly to the Lord, and will trust Him perfectly, we shall find our souls "mounting up with wings as eagles" to the "heavenly places" in Christ Jesus, where earthly annoyances or sorrows have no power to disturb us.[3]

Smith goes on to point out that just as a bird needs both wings to fly, we need both qualities of surrender and trust to fly like the eagle.

It is a sad thing to see a bird hopping along, flapping one wing in an effort to fly. No matter how hard it tries, a bird with a broken or clipped wing cannot get off the ground. The same is true for us. If either wing of surrender or trust is broken, then no matter how hard we work, we cannot mature spiritually, and we are more vulnerable to attack from the Enemy of our souls.

How does one without the other disable us spiritually? Surrender without trust leads to fatalism. Trust without surrender produces a person who seeks to maintain control over their situation.

Having lived and worked among Muslims for thirteen years, we have seen the effects of surrender without trust. The word Islam actually comes from the Arabic word *aslama*, which means to surrender or resign oneself. When a child dies and the mother wails in anguish, her husband curtly tells her to be quiet, because she must accept the will of Allah.

Muslims submit to Allah, but they cannot trust Him. To them, God is an impersonal deity who is approached from a distance and served out of fear rather than love. After a lifetime of trying to gain God's favor by following the rules of faith, even the most devout Muslims can be turned away at the door of heaven at the whim of a capricious Allah. There is no Savior to put an arm around them and say, "I have bought them with my blood. They're in on Me." There is no relationship, nothing to inspire hope or joy.

On the other hand, trying to trust without surrender is disabling because we try to keep control of our lives. This produces an attitude that says, "I trust You, God. I know You can do all things—and here is how I want You to do it." Trust without surrender leads to a controlling approach to life, devoid of true rest.

We cannot rest as long as we feel it is up to us to make life work. We attempt to control God with our prayers, or even with our confusion and anger, rather than rest when life does not work out as we expect. We wonder what God is doing. We wonder why He is not answering our prayers, especially when we ask for good things.

Sometimes God answers yes, and at other times His answer is no. The yes answers are wonderful and bring a smile to our face and somersaults in our heart. The no answers, if we are honest, are less wonderful. If we had wanted the answer to be no, we would not have asked. But sulking only reveals our shallow trust.

Amy Carmichael shared these thoughts in *Rose from Brier*:

It is a petty view of our Father's love and wisdom which demands or expects an answer according to our desires, apart from His wisdom. We see hardly one inch of the narrow lane of time. To our God eternity lies open as a meadow. It must seem strange to the heavenly people who have seen the beautiful End of the Lord, that we should ever question what Love allows to be, or call a prayer "unanswered" when the answer is not what we expect.[4]

I have learned in thirty years of walking with God that
He knows better than I what the answer to my prayers should
be. He is far wiser than I,
and He has the eagle's point
of view. D.L. Moody sums
up prayer that flies on the
wings of surrender and
trust like this: "Spread out
your petition before God,
and then say, 'Thy will be
done.' The sweetest lesson I have learned in God's school is
to let the Lord choose for me."[5]

*When we surrender and
trust, we find the joy and
peace of a heart at rest.*

Fatalism submits to the will of a distant and capricious
God. A controlling attitude demands our own way. But when
we surrender *and* trust, we find the joy of relationship with
our God and the peace of a heart at rest.

We are not fatalists, nor are we demanding servants. We
are sons and daughters of a King. We surrender to a Father
who pulls us into His embrace and whom we can trust for
our good.

Trusting Surrender

Louis was well known where we lived in Chad, because
for some years he was the only doctor in the region. As an
expatriate doctor he had many patients outside the hospital,
including the grandson of a king—or rather a sultan, as he
would be called in Chad.

Although Chad now has a president and civil authorities, sultans still maintain a presence among the people. The
sultan of the Ouaddai region where we lived still wielded a
powerful influence in matters of traditional and religious law.

The sultan's grandson, Louis's patient, was a delightful boy of eight years old who lived at the palace with his family. Imagine a large mud-brick and cement building, white-washing inside and out, carpets covering cement floors and satellite dishes on the roof, and you have the picture of a palace Chadian style. Louis made regular visits to this home to provide treatment, usually seeing only the princess and her son.

After one visit, however, he was summoned to speak with the sultan. Immensely curious to see the Chadian version of a throne room, Louis walked across the dirt courtyard, took off his shoes according to protocol and placed them with the many others outside the entrance. He stepped into a spacious room lined wall-to-wall with ornate carpets.

At the far end was the sultan, a large man seated cross-legged on the floor, robed and turbaned. Groups of people, waiting to speak with him, sat on the carpet at various distances from the revered man. Louis was familiar enough with the culture to know that location indicated status, and he could not help but notice that women and children were lined up at the back. The rest of the room was filled with men in scattered small groups.

There is a reason, apparently, for this carefully observed etiquette in the sultan's presence. We had recently visited the ruins of the ancient Ouaddian sultanate and learned that in ancient times, those who approached the sultan in even the most remotely improper way were beheaded. Louis could not help but think of this as he stepped through the door. He was thankful times had changed.

Still, there was a code of conduct to follow. Louis stood barefoot at the entrance of the room and waited. When the sultan beckoned, he moved forward a few steps, and then stopped. When he beckoned again, Louis moved a few more steps and stopped again, never assuming he had the right to approach at his own discretion. Despite the seriousness of the visit, Louis kept thinking of the game "red light, green light" as he inched forward bit by bit at the sultan's command.

Because of his status as a physician, Louis was summoned all the way to the front, where he sat cross-legged on the carpet and conversed with the sultan about the grandson's treatment. As they were speaking, something happened that Louis has never forgotten.

A noise at the back of the room and the sultan's diverted attention made Louis turn his head in time to see the grandson running across the carpet. Shoes on his feet and ignoring all convention, the little boy ran to the front of the room and jumped into his grandfather's open arms. The sultan wrapped his arms around the boy, who settled in for the remainder of the conversation.

Like the sultan's grandson, we too have the status of sons and daughters of God (see John 1:12) with all the rights and privileges it allows. The wings of surrender and trust are the means of lifting us into joy and rest in relationship with our own Father.

Taking God at His Word

As children of God, we serve a Father whose Word can be trusted:

> Your word, O LORD, is eternal;
>   it stands firm in the heavens.
> Your faithfulness continues through all generations;
>   you established the earth, and it endures. (Ps. 119:89–90)

God's word to us is that He is good, and what He does is good (see Ps. 119:68), that all His ways are loving and faithful (see Ps. 25:10) and that He works everything in our life for our good (see Rom. 8:28). The wing of surrender is strengthened by our relationship with God and rises with joy and hope. The wing of trust is strengthened by the promises of God and rises with peace and rest. If we do not believe God means what He says, then we cannot rest on His promises.

> *If we do not believe God means what He says, then we cannot rest on His promises.*

Fénelon observed that "it is easy to say to oneself, 'I love God with all my heart,' when conscious of nothing but pleasure in such love. But true love is that which suffers while loving: 'Though he slay me, yet will I hope in him'!" (Job 13:15).[6]

"The wings of the soul," writes Hannah Whitall Smith, "carry it up into a spiritual plane of life, into the 'life hid with Christ in God,' which is life utterly independent of circumstances, one that no cage can imprison and no shackles bind."[7]

Abdel-nabi is a young Chadian man who used his wings of surrender and trust to soar above his circumstances.

His sister had committed a crime, and she needed a large sum of money to pay a court fine for her offense. So to pay her fine, she sold Abdel-nabi's land. When he protested her actions in a local court and tried to recover his land, he was told that because he had become a Christian, he had lost his right to inherit the land his father had given as a Muslim. It was no longer his, so his sister could take it for her own use.

Our mission team prayed fervently and boldly with

Abdel-nabi, asking God to overrule the authorities. But even though he made several appearances before the court in an effort to gain back his land, the response was always the same.

It was becoming clear that God was not going to move the authorities to change their minds. We felt like the psalmist who complained that the wicked get away with everything, while the innocent suffer (see Ps. 73:1–17).

One morning Abdel-nabi showed up at our house with excitement on his face. He had read of "an inheritance that can never perish, spoil or fade—kept in heaven for you" (1 Pet. 1:4) and knew that God was speaking about his situation. He was not to worry about his earthly inheritance any longer.

"Every acceptance of his will becomes an altar of sacrifice," Hannah Hurnard continues in her introduction, "and every such surrender and abandonment of ourselves to his will is a means of furthering us on the way to the High Places to which he desires to bring every child of his while they are still living on earth."[8]

This was true for Abdel-nabi. We could see the change in the following days when he showed genuine peace and a deeper joy than we had seen in him before. He took God at His word, accepted His will and soared to the heights with the eagles.

He did make a final trip to the courtroom, however. This time it was to tell the Islamic authorities, "My sister can have the land. I don't need it, because I have an inheritance waiting for me in heaven that will never be taken away." Through surrender and trust in a difficult situation, Abdel-nabi found hope and peace in his heart.

God does not promise escape from our difficulties; He promises, rather, hope and strength to rise above them. Both are connected to our inner, hidden life and not to outward, visible events. *Hope in the Lord*, Isaiah wrote, is what renews our strength.

Hannah Whitall Smith gives a beautiful summary of a soul that is hoping in the Lord:

> What are the chief characteristics of this life hid with Christ in God, and how [does it] differ from much in the ordinary Christian life? Its chief characteristics are an entire surrender to the Lord, and a perfect trust in Him, resulting in victory over sin and inward rest of soul; and it differs from the lower range of Christian experience in that it causes us to let the Lord carry our burdens and manage our affairs for us instead of trying to do it ourselves.[9]

My desires, hopes, fears, struggles, possessions, relationships, finances . . . Jesus tells me to give Him every one of these so He can give me all of Himself in return. I have to trust He will be all I need; then my soul can discover its deepest security and satisfaction.

Heart Beats

Cannot you see that it is mere folly to be afraid of giving ourselves too entirely to God? It merely means that we are afraid of being too happy, of accepting his will in all things too heartily, of bearing our inevitable trials too bravely, of finding too much rest in his love, of letting go too easily the worldly passions which make us miserable. . . . We would [instead] be full of trust, and looking forward to eternal blessings would comfort us for the earthly happiness which seems to slip from under our feet. God's love would give wings to our feet in treading his paths and lifting us up beyond all our care. If you doubt me, try this Scripture: "Taste and see that the LORD is good" (Ps. 34:8)! (*François Fénelon*)[10]

The heart that listens:

During the next few days meditate on the following passages of Scripture. Ask God to speak to you about surrender and trust in circumstances.

2 Samuel 22:7
Psalm 27:13–14
Psalm 33:13–22
Isaiah 41:10

Read Luke 9:23–26. Ask God to speak to you about surrender and trust in your relationship with Him.

Giving up something that we can't attain anyway is not self-denial. Nor is giving up things we don't want in the first place. True self-denial for Christ's sake means denying ourselves something we want and can have—but for His sake, we say no. How are absolute surrender and absolute trust necessary for restoring us to the image of Christ?

The heart that responds:

What do you need to surrender in order to live more fully for Christ? Mentally take each thing the Lord shows you to the foot of the cross and leave it there, trusting Him to work in your circumstances and in you for His glory.

Epilogue

And now, Lord, with your help, I will become myself. (*Soren Kierkegaard*)

And we, who with unveiled faces all reflect the Lord's glory, are
being transformed into His likeness with ever-increasing glory,
which comes from the Lord, who is the Spirit.
(*2 Corinthians 3:18*)

You and I were created to belong to God, to be loved by
Him and to be His image bearers. Robert McGee wrote in
The Search for Significance, "If we know who we are, we will
not try to become someone else in order to have value and
meaning in our lives. If we don't know who we are, we will
try to become someone who someone else wants us to be!"[1]

Sin broke our soul's connection with God, destroyed our
capacity to be image bearers and made us forget who we are.
It turned us into image projectors, the ultimate of becoming
what someone else wants us to be in order to have value and
meaning.

But sin did not destroy God's love for us or His commitment to our restoration. Through Jesus' death, the power of
sin was broken at the cross, and our souls can once more
find their way home. Through Jesus' life and the transforming power of the Spirit, the image of God can once more be
restored in us. These truths alone make us soar to the heights
if we will live by them.

When Jesus calls us to absolute loyalty to His person, absolute obedience to His standards and absolute surrender to His will, His purpose is to reverse the results of the Fall and make restoration possible. I must believe I can entrust myself to Christ's strong love.

When the branch surrenders to the life of the vine rather than striving to produce fruit on its own, the fruit comes. Christ life inwardly experienced will lead to Christlikeness outwardly expressed. "All God's love and the fruits of it come to us as we are in Christ, and are one with him," wrote Richard Sibbes, an English theologian in the seventeenth century. The key is our oneness with Him.

The wings of surrender and trust enable us to rise above our circumstances and discover another point of view that helps us make sense of them. We defy the downward pull of self-effort and rise from "churchianity" to following Christ, from false fruit to the real thing, from image projecting to image bearing, from a soul that strives to a soul that rests. We become who we are meant to be.

Endnotes

Dedication Page

1. Amy Carmichael, "The Last Defile" in *Mountain Breezes* (Fort Washington, PA: CLC Publications, 1999), p. 102.

Letter to the Reader

1. Antoine de Saint-Exupéry, source unknown.

Chapter 1: Engagements of the Heart

1. To be fair to all pastors and Sunday School teachers who are faithfully speaking these truths, I now know that I heard them throughout my childhood, but I was listening with my head only. Only when I listened with my heart did I truly arrive at a point of sincere response.
2. *The Hebrew-Greek Keyword Study Bible: New International Version* (Chattanooga: AMG International, Inc., 1995).

Part Two (Title Page)

1. Oswald Chambers, *My Utmost for His Highest* (Uhrichsville, OH: Barbour, 1935), p. 8.

Chapter 2: Surrendering

1. R.C. Sproul at Tentmaker Ministries (accessed January 2009), http://www.tentmaker.org/Quotes/keys.htm.
2. Nearly $29 million as compared to share of GDP. See Measuring Worth (accessed January 2009), http://www.measuringworth.com/ukcompare/.
3. Chambers, *My Utmost for His Highest*, p. 97.
4. Dietrich Bonhoeffer, *The Cost of Discipleship* (New York: MacMillan, 1963), p. 64.

Chapter 3: Treasuring

1. C.S. Lewis, *Poems*, ed. Walter Hooper (New York: Harcourt Brace Jovanovich, 1964), p. 110.
2. Lilias Trotter, *Focussed: A Story and a Song* in Miriam Huffman Rockness, *A Passion for the Impossible* (Grand Rapids: Discovery House Publishers, 2003), pp. 332–333.
3. Thomas Doolittle, *The New Encyclopedia of Christian Quotations* (Grand Rapids: Baker Books, 2000), p. 645.

Chapter 4: Emptying

1. Max Lucado, *It's Not About Me* (Nashville: Integrity Publishers, 2004), p. 5.
2. Ralph Waldo Emerson in Paul Marshall with Lela Gilbert, *Heaven Is Not My Home: Living in the Now of God's Creation* (Nashville: Word Publishing, 1998), p. 195.
3. Richard Rolle, *The Fire of Love* (New York: Viking Penquin, 1972).

4. Amy Carmichael, *Edges of His Ways* (Fort Washington, PA: CLC Publications, 1955), p. 132.
5. Evan Roberts in James A. Stewart, *Invasion of Wales by the Spirit through Evan Roberts* (Asheville, NC: Revival Literature, 1963), p. 60.
6. François Fénelon, *The Royal Way of the Cross*, ed. Hall M. Helms (Brewster, MA: Paraclete Press, 1982).
7. François Fénelon, *The Best of Fénelon: Spiritual Letters, Christian Counsel, Maxims of the Saints,* ed. Harold J. Chadwick (Gainesville, FL: Bridge-Logos, 2002), p. 16.
8. This form of prayer is adapted from Sylvia Gunter's excellent material on prayer. See The Father's Business, P.O. Box 380333, Birmingham, AL 35238, www.thefathersbusiness.com.

Chapter 5: Entering

1. Paul Shepard, *Man in the Landscape: A Historic View of the Esthetics of Nature* (Athens, GA: University of Georgia Press, 2002).
2. Madame Jeanne Guyon, *A Short and Very Easy Method of Prayer,* now titled *Experiencing the Depths of Jesus Christ,* trans. Gene Edwards (Sargent, GA: SeedSowers Christian Books Publishing, 1975), p. 118.
3. Ibid. p. 45.
4. Evelyn Underhill in *NIV Classics Devotional Bible: With Daily Readings from Men and Women Whose Faith Influenced the World* (Grand Rapids, Zondervan, 1996), p. 1238.
5. Rosalind Rinker, *Prayer: Conversing with God* (Grand Rapids: Zondervan, 1959), p. 23.

6. Jeff Lucas, *Elijah: Anointed and Stressed* (Colorado Springs: David C. Cook, 1998) p. 128.

Chapter 6: Remaining

1. Amy Carmichael, *Rose from Brier* (Fort Washington, PA: CLC Publications, 1980), p. 151.
2. Matthew Henry, *The Secret of Communion with God* (Grand Rapids: Kregel, 1991), p. 9.
3. Guyon, *Experiencing the Depths of Jesus Christ*, p. 65.

Chapter 7: Seeing

1. Dan DeHaan, *The God You Can Know* (Chicago: Moody Press, 1992), p. 28.
2. A.B. Simpson, quoted in the *NIV Classics Devotional Bible* (Grand Rapids: Zondervan, 1996), p. 615.
3. George MacDonald, *Diary of an Old Soul* (Minneapolis: Augsburg Fortress, 1994), pp. 96–97.

Chapter 8: Believing

1. Dallas Willard, *The Divine Conspiracy: Rediscovering our Hidden Life in God* (San Francisco: Harper, 1998), p. 307.
2. Ibid. p. 315.
3. E.M. Bounds, *E.M. Bounds: The Classic Collection on Prayer*, ed. Harold Chadwick (Gainesville, FL: Bridge-Logos, 1997), p. 51.
4. From the workshop materials of Ken Williams, Ph.D, *Sharpening Your Interpersonal Skills* (Colorado Springs: International Training Partners, Inc., 2002), p. 3.

5. Ibid. p. 37. The concept of the "bubble" as an indicator of something hidden below the surface is also used in International Training Partners' materials on effective listening.

6. Martha Kilpatrick, "Martha vs. Mary" in *Adoration* (Jacksonville: Seedsowers, 1999), p. 17.

7. DeHaan, *The God You Can Know*, p. 17.

Chapter 9: Soaring

1. F.B. Meyer, *Christ in Isaiah* (London: Blundell House, 1970), p. 23.

2. Hannah Hurnard, *Hinds Feet on High Places* (Wheaton, IL: Tyndale, 1975), pp. 10–11.

3. Hannah Whitall Smith, *The Christian's Secret of a Happy Life* (Grand Rapids: Revell, 1974), p. 167.

4. Amy Carmichael, *Rose from Brier*, pp. 155–156.

5. D.L. Moody, source unknown.

6. Fénelon, *The Royal Way of the Cross*, ed. Hall M. Helms, p. 108.

7. Smith, *The Christian's Secret of a Happy Life*, p. 167.

8. Hurnard, *Hinds Feet on High Places*, p. 12.

9. Smith, *The Christian's Secret of a Happy Life*, p. 28.

10. Fénelon, *The Royal Way of the Cross*, ed. Hall M. Helms, p. 61.

Epilogue

1. Robert S. McGee, *The Search for Significance* (Thomas Nelson, 1998), p. 46.

This book was produced by CLC Publications. We hope it has been life-changing and has given you a fresh experience of God through the work of the Holy Spirit. CLC Publications is an outreach of CLC Ministries International, a global literature mission with work in over 50 countries. If you would like to know more about us or are interested in opportunities to serve with a faith mission, we invite you to contact us at:

CLC Ministries International
P.O. Box 1449
Fort Washington, PA 19034

_____

Phone: (215) 542-1242
E-mail: orders@clcpublications.com
Website: www.clcpublications.com

- -

DO YOU LOVE GOOD CHRISTIAN BOOKS?
Do you have a heart for worldwide missions?

You can receive a FREE subscription to *HeartBeat*, CLC's newsletter on global literature missions.

Order by e-mail at:
clcheartbeat@clcusa.org

Or fill in the coupon below and mail to:
P.O. Box 1449
Fort Washington, PA 19034

┌ - - - - - - - - - - - - - - - - - - - ┐

FREE *HEARTBEAT* SUBSCRIPTION!

Name: _____

Address: _____

_____

Phone: _____ E-mail: _____

└ - - - - - - - - - - - - - - - - - - - ┘

READ THE REMARKABLE STORY OF
the founding of
CLC International

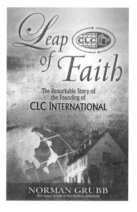